# Bright Lights of the Second City

50 Prominent Chicagoans on Living with Passion and Purpose

12/24/14

Dear Nancy,
Let your bright lights Shine!
Warm wishes,
Betsy

# Bright Lights of the Second City

50 Prominent Chicagoans on Living with Passion and Purpose

by

**Betsy Storm**

Top
Drawer

# Top
# Drawer

Top Drawer Communications LLC

Chicago, Illinois


www.topdrawercommunications.com

Cover Design by Trisect Design, Glen Ellyn, Illinois

Interior Design by Merle Welkomer, Chicago, Illinois

Typesetting by Network Publishing Partners, Glenview, Illinois

Printed in the United States of America by Color House Graphics, Grand Rapids, Michigan


Library of Congress Control Number:  2014936475

# Contents

# Acknowledgments

I am grateful to have an array of wise and thoughtful friends. I tip my hat to each for the many occasions she generously brainstormed, read drafts, and bolstered me with support and encouragement – especially Paula Poda, Leslie Storm, Carol Woodworth, Edie Kasten, Barb Granner, Marilyn Soglin, Helene Huffer, Jennifer Lyng Rueff, Amy Krause, Joen Kinnan, Lauri Sanders, Katie Truesdell, and Beth Russo.

My husband, Jack, listened to endless hours of self-talk as I worked through the process of writing a book, and his contributions enhanced the final product. Katie and Colin, my adult children, embody the passion and purpose that fills and refills me.

I offer endless thanks to Bill Storm, my newspaper reporter Dad. Although he is no longer physically with me, his spirited commitment to storytelling accompanies me daily.

Next, bouquets of affection to Reverend Elizabeth Andrews, a spiritual advisor and friend who nourishes so many seekers with her bold spirit, sparkling intelligence, and faithful support of their dreams and aspirations.

Linda Wolf of Network Publishing Partners guided me (aka Alice) confidently through The Looking Glass World that is self-publishing.

Last, there wouldn't *be* any *Bright Lights of the Second City* without the generosity of the fifty stellar Chicagoans you will come to know in these pages. Without exception, they shared their personal stories thoughtfully, frankly, and in great detail. I selected these individuals, in large part, because they live in a fashion that inspires and motivates me to reach beyond my grasp on a daily basis. I am so impressed by the remarkable traits they share – particularly a dedication to their art, science, mission, sport, or craft; dogged tenacity; and willingness to live boldly. Their collective contributions make our world-class city, and our world, a more compassionate, interesting, intelligent, artful, and gracious place to call home.

# Introduction

*I think the purpose of life is . . . above all, to matter, to count, to stand for something,*
*to have made some difference that you lived at all.*
– Leo Rosten, Russian-born writer

High achievers – by definition, individuals fueled by passion and purpose – distinguish themselves through exceptional contributions. These luminaries often share extraordinary work ethics, rare degrees of commitment, and a devotion to specific ideals that define their callings. Importantly, many credit a specific person, life situation, or incident with igniting a rare belief in their abilities to create lives of meaning and self-determination.

*Bright Lights of the Second City* details the remarkable stories of life-altering experiences that shaped the characters and careers of these Chicago leaders across the arenas of activism, the arts, business, philanthropy, politics, science, spirituality, sports, and more.

In-depth, one-on-one interviews describe the life journeys and insights of fifty prominent Chicagoans – in their own words. You will discover the experiences that led to excellence in a favorite athlete, inspired a much-admired theatrical figure to rise to the top in one of the world's most competitive professions, and shaped the determination of a world-class financier.

Is it possible to identify the motivations that enliven these movers and shakers, these midnight-oil burners who pursue their dreams with true grit and then often make their accomplishments look easy? (Ah, if the outside world only knew. . . .) The answer: a resounding *yes*.

Each person was asked an individualized series of questions, depending on his or her field of expertise. Among them were the following:

- What kind of "crucible moments" forged your development and character?

- Who inspired you to follow your passion, and how?

- What books, films, or music would you recommend to renew the spirit and inspire the soul?

- What advice would you offer to someone seeking success in your field, or simply in the quest for a more fulfilling life?

- Who are your favorite poets and performers?

- What places in Chicago and beyond have given you a peaceful interlude or are especially important to you?

- What quotations hold special significance for you? (At the bottom of this page is one of my personal favorites from "Someone Digging in the Ground" by Rumi, a thirteenth-century Persian poet.)

During the time I spent writing this book, I felt as if I attended graduate school for free – an advanced education in "a life well-lived" by fifty Chicagoans whose contributions to our city are as diverse as the neighborhoods that help define us. I hope their stories will move you as they did me.

*"The soul exists for its own joy."*

This book is dedicated to my special string of illuminators,
each a bright bulb that shines a light on
how a successful blended family is created.
And especially to Jack, for every little thing he does
to make our lives happy ones.

# Carol Adams

CEO, DuSable Museum of
African American History

"If you don't know African history, you don't
know American history," she reminds us.

*After a long and storied career in academia and public service, Carol Adams, Ph.D., now presides over the DuSable★ Museum of African American History, the first and oldest museum dedicated to the study and conservation of African American history, culture, and art. In several years, when a "new" building – the renovated 1880 Roundhouse designed by renowned Chicago architect and urban planner Daniel Burnham – is annexed right across the street from DuSable's 57th Street location in Hyde Park, DuSable will also be the largest museum of its kind. A sociologist with the requisite affinity for research, Adams has held positions as Chairman of African Studies at Loyola University and Director of the Center for Inner City Studies at Northeastern Illinois University. Two entrepreneurial ventures she helped develop to foster trade and economic development in Africa are typical of her community-building endeavors, Made in Africa and BUTTA (Bringing You the Treasures of Africa).*

*Continually seeking new ways to help herself and other African Americans better understand their identities, Adams recently learned – using newly discovered DNA knowledge – that her roots are from the Northern Nigerian branch of the Fulani people, an ethnic group spread over many countries, predominantly in West Africa. She intends to encourage other African Americans to undertake their personal genealogies, and has even incorporated such DNA testing into DuSable's annual arts and crafts festival. Adams also is a former Secretary of the Illinois Department of Human Services. She received her bachelor's degree at Nashville's Fisk University and then pursued graduate work at Boston University, University of Chicago, and Union Graduate School.*

I was fortunate to grow up in the same Louisville, Kentucky, neighborhood where my father had lived all of his life. He was the circulation manager for the *Louisville Times* and *Courier Journal* newspapers, and we did well economically. A huge "giver backer," he taught us that even though our family could have afforded to move to a more affluent community, we didn't . . . because it isn't right to just walk away and leave your roots behind you. Instead, you stay around and make a difference.

One of the pivotal moments in my life came early on, at age fifteen, when I was arrested after participating in my first civil rights march. My mother worried that the arrest would be problematic for my father's job, but rather, he told me how proud he was that I'd stood up for my beliefs. I was fortunate to have strong family support; several of my friends were forbidden to demonstrate because their families feared repercussions.

A key lesson he'd learned while attending Tuskegee University, one of the nation's top historically African American universities, was that it was essential to "have your own" – a source of income beyond a regular job. My dad always had businesses on the side, which provided us all with a sense of freedom. He taught me you should never be afraid to speak out for your beliefs for fear of losing a job. That lesson has helped me throughout my life and, as a young woman, it validated my actions.

My serious learning about the importance of Africa as the cradle of civilization began when I started teaching at Northeastern Illinois University's Center for Inner City Studies in 1968. Through my exposure to other scholars, I developed a different, broader way of looking at the world and my place in it. One of the most meaningful books that has shaped my thinking throughout my career is *The Mis-Education of the Negro* by Carter Woodson [published in 1933]. It explains the role education has played in maintaining the status quo for African Americans for many, many years – particularly making the point that keeping our history from us is a powerful way of ensuring that African Americans continue to feel inferior. When you don't know about your identity and where you came from, that lack of knowledge impedes the development of positive identity and self-worth.

The DuSable Museum is now fifty-five years old [as of 2012], and my goal is to position us for a successful, sustainable future. Our co-founder, Dr. Margaret Burroughs, is the person I most admire. She realized it was important to institutionalize the work of preserving and showcasing African American culture, so she took on the huge challenge of starting the museum. Dr. Burroughs is a wonderful example of the importance of taking positive action rather than just complaining about the status quo. Chicago is a city rich in African American history. The museum is named for Jean Baptiste Pointe DuSable, a Haitian of African and French descent. In 1779, he established the trading post and permanent settlement that eventually became known as Chicago.

The museum will continue to develop its role as a vital venue for important conversations in the city of Chicago. For example, a recent series titled "DuSable Museum Means Business" focused on economics and the African community. We're also partnering with the Court Theater at the University of Chicago and the Botanic Garden in Highland Park – among other organizations – to expose new audiences to the museum. Our education initiatives include digitizing our collection so that the museum's extensive resources will be accessible to anyone. We want people to know and celebrate the contributions of African Americans to this community. If you don't know African history, you don't know American history.

*Carol Adams was interviewed on July 10, 2012, at the DuSable Museum. Her birthday is May 11.*

## Favorites

**BOOK**

*The Warmth of Other Suns: The Epic Story of America's Great Migration* by Isabel Wilkerson. A historical study, the book tells the story of the six million African Americans who moved away from the South to start new – and unknown – lives in other regions of the United States.

**PERFORMERS**

Singers Dianne Reeves and Lalah Hathaway.

**POEM**

"I am a Black Woman" by Mari Evans. Its message is empowering, strong, and beautiful. Here are the closing lines:

"impervious
indestructible
Look on me and be renewed"

**QUOTATION**

"Without struggle, there is no progress."
    – FREDERICK DOUGLASS, AFRICAN AMERICAN SOCIAL REFORMER, ORATOR, WRITER, AND STATESMAN

★ Jean Baptiste Point DuSable, the museum's namesake, is regarded as the first permanent resident of the area that later became Chicago. In addition to the museum, a school, harbor, park, and bridge have been named, or renamed, in his honor. The place where DuSable settled at the mouth of the Chicago River in the 1780s is recognized as a National Historic Landmark.

66 *Without struggle, there is no progress.* 99

Photo by John McArthur

# Lori Andrews

## Bioethicist

Making new law for a new era, she combines legal and ethical wisdom and laces it with compassion.

*A bioethicist★ and biotechnology expert, Lori Andrews, J.D., reigns as an internationally recognized voice on emerging technologies and the seismic ethical questions such advancements inevitably usher in. Like a modern-day town crier, she spotlights the potential menaces that haunt hot-button issues such as Internet privacy and human cloning. Andrews is a Distinguished Professor of Law at Illinois Institute of Technology (IIT) Chicago-Kent, Director of the Illinois Institute of Technology's Institute for Science, Law and Technology, and an Associate Vice President of the Illinois Institute of Technology.*

*Andrews has authored more than a dozen books, both nonfiction and fiction. Her most recent title is* I Know Who You Are and I Saw What You Did: Social Networks and the Death of Privacy. *She makes frequent media appearances, including those on "60 Minutes," "Good Morning America," and "Oprah."*

*Andrews earned her B.A. and her J.D. at Yale College and Yale Law School, respectively.* USA Today *said of her: "When octuplets are born in Houston, when a dead man fathers a baby in Los Angeles, when 'twins' of different races are born after a medical mix-up, whom are you going to call? Andrews is definitely on the short list." In her opinion, the three words that epitomize Andrews are driven, compassionate, and unstoppable.*

My dad was a pharmacist and Mom was a homemaker with a streak of willingness to question authority, which I inherited. Our dinner table was a place of interesting conversation. From early on, it seemed to me that if something went wrong, there ought to be a remedy. When my Ken doll went bald, I complained to Mattel and they sent me a new head.

I was bored at school as a kid until fourth grade, when my teacher in Bellwood, Mrs. Peller, decided to gather a group of high-testing students who would attend regular school for a half day then spend the rest of the day with her going on field trips, conducting independent, in-depth research on topics of our choice, and writing reports on them. Every year, about twenty of us would travel someplace exciting, like Denver or New York City. As a result of missing regular classes, I know none of the state capitols, but learned to love writing, research, and travel from an early age. By age sixteen, I started selling articles to publications.

When I arrived at Yale College as part of only the second class that included women [graduating in 1975], a big banner proclaimed they were going to train "1000 male leaders a year." In college and at Yale Law School, I wrote about social issues from unions to medical care. The male focus at Yale was inadvertently helpful in preparing for my summer job as the only woman among twenty associates at a prestigious New York City law firm.

The event that launched my career was an invitation to speak in Germany at the First World Conference on in-vitro fertilization in 1981, followed by testimony before the U.S. Congress. Interestingly, I passed the bar exam in 1978 on the birthday of Louise Brown, the first "test tube baby." When the reality of cloning and embryo research surfaced, many people thought they were marginal issues, which of course they weren't. I was asked for advice by both a Democratic president, Bill Clinton, and a Republican president, George W. Bush, about cloning-related controversies.

One of the challenges of being a bioethicist is that while science is always looking forward, the law looks back. I'm interested in the areas where the law has not yet caught up with medical technology. People say, "If there's no existing law, call her."

The U.S. Constitution is the most significant piece of writing I know. It's stood the test of time and remained flexible and fluid, in part because it was created by politician-philosophers who sensed what is essential for human beings to flourish.

I find myself most inspired not by any one person, but by individuals who overcome amazing odds – like homeless people who are admitted to Harvard and those who struggle daily just to make ends meet. Those people are my heroes.

*Lori Andrews was interviewed on May 8, 2012, at her office at IIT Chicago-Kent College of Law in the Loop. She was born in September 1952.*

---

# Favorites

**BOOKS**
Any of Michael Crichton's books – they all open the door to let people peer inside scientific laboratories.

**MOVIE**
*Blade Runner* (1982), directed by Ridley Scott. The film inspires people to think about where our technologies are taking us.

**NONPROFIT**
The March of Dimes. The organization advances science and medicine while keeping bioethics in mind.

**PLACE**
National Veterans Art Museum in Chicago. A visit here inspires greater understanding of the real impact of war with a focus on Vietnam. Through this place, people find a way to cope with tragedy through art.

**QUOTATION**
"The world is a fine place, and worth the fighting for."
– ERNEST HEMINGWAY, AMERICAN WRITER

---

* Dictionary.com defines bioethics as a field of study concerned with the ethical and philosophical implications of certain biological and medical procedures, technologies, and treatments, such as organ transplants, genetic engineering, and care of the terminally ill. Lori Andrews adds, "It's about making choices that fundamentally change our society. The ethics aspect of it explores the question, 'What will our world look like if a specific law or technology is enacted?'"

"*...worth the fighting for.*"

# Stephen Asma

## Philosophy Professor and Buddhist

He enlightens readers about how Buddhism gives one greater control over one's life – without turning to the "magical thinking" found in many religions.

*Stephen Asma, Ph.D., began teaching at Columbia College in 1994. He earned his B.A. in philosophy at Northern Illinois University and a Ph.D. in philosophy at Southern Illinois University. He has authored seven books, including* Buddha for Beginners; The Gods Drink Whiskey: Stumbling Toward Enlightenment in the Land of the Tattered Buddha; Why I am a Buddhist: No-Nonsense Buddhism with Red Meat and Whiskey; *and* Against Fairness.

*Appointed the first Distinguished Scholar of Columbia College by the Provost (2006-2008), Asma regularly contributes to the Chicago Public Radio program "848." Born in Waukegan, Illinois, and the son of a steelworker, he has lived in Phnom Penh City, Cambodia, and Shanghai, China, and has traveled extensively in Thailand, Laos, and Vietnam, among other Asian countries.*

I grew up attending Catholic school and was an altar boy and a lector. In eighth grade, a priest who occasionally visited our classroom talked to us about people like Aristotle and Saint Thomas Aquinas. He asked a lot of interesting questions using Aristotelian analysis, and I thought to myself, "This is the stuff for me." The priest emphasized that, "Here are a lot of interesting questions that we don't know the answers to, but a lot of smart people are thinking about them." I didn't know it at the time, but he was talking about philosophy.

I soon began reading the works of Aldous Huxley and Thomas Merton, the go-betweens of Western and Eastern spiritual traditions. Then, as I learned more and more about Hinduism, Daoism, Buddhism, and other religions, I came to think of Catholicism as providing too small a pond for my interests in spirituality; it is provincial and narrow in terms of ideas, such as good versus evil. Look at the Bible, for example. It's a set of stories in which certain values are enshrined while others are simply left out.

My way of thinking about human beings was massively transformed by reading Charles Darwin. Prior to Darwin, people thought of the mind, for example, as a miracle given to humans by God. To the contrary, Darwin explained that the mind was a product of nature. The evolutionary way of thinking challenges us to rethink the higher dimensions of ourselves – such as our ethical sense and desire to help others.

Rather than claim our gifts are miracles "sent from above," Buddhism teaches a more adult form of spirituality. It asks: How can we better weather the challenges of everyday experiences rather than throw holy water on the problems? In so doing, it attempts to give human beings greater control over their lives and spirits without turning to the magical thinking – involving miracles, mysteries, and authority figures – found in many religions. I believe that to be the most juvenile, childlike kind of spirituality.

At the start of his odyssey, the Buddha was particularly struggling to solve the problem of how to alleviate suffering. After studying with Hindu masters and becoming very ascetic for several years, he had acquired great discipline but it had not helped him with his questions about suffering. Later, he made one of his greatest contributions – a development he considered to be the pathway to wisdom, known as *The Middle Way*. It's a path of moderation between the extremes of hedonistic indulgence and total self-denial.

Buddhism is practiced differently around the world, and it doesn't have to involve the formalities of attending a temple or practicing regular sitting meditation, though it often does. Many people, including myself, practice Buddhism through mindfulness, or insight and meditation. You can practice it in the here and now, whether you're playing an instrument or cleaning the house. The importance of being in the present moment is that it makes you more attuned to what's happening in the world. You can gain heightened awareness of others' needs and, as you continue to practice, you can become more compassionate. Metaphorically speaking, the present moment is all we have.

*Stephen Asma was interviewed on October 4, 2010, at his academic office at Columbia College on Michigan Avenue in Chicago. His birthday is July 2, 1966.*

---

## Favorites

**BOOK**
*What the Buddha Taught* by Dr. Walpola Rahula. *The Journal of the Buddhist Society* said of this title, "Authoritative and clear, logical and sober, this study is as comprehensive as it is masterly."

**MOVIE**
*The Scent of Green Papaya* (1993), directed by Tran Anh Hung. In reviewing this Vietnamese film, critic Roger Ebert praised, "It's like seeing a poem for the eyes."

**MUSIC**
Jazz and other improvisational music, especially by performers Miles Davis and slide guitarist Ry Cooder.

**POET**
Matsuo Basho, Japanese haiku poet.

**QUOTATION**
"But all things excellent are as difficult as they are rare."
    – BENEDICT DE SPINOZA, SEVENTEENTH-CENTURY DUTCH PHILOSOPHER

"*...as difficult as they are rare.*"

Photo by Hal Baim

# Tracy Baim

## LGBT Activist and Journalist

Helping to ensure Chicago remains a
world-class city for the LGBT Community,
she applies her journalistic talents across a
variety of platforms.

*Tracy Baim is a Chicago-based journalist and publisher of the award-winning* Windy
City Times *newspaper. Since age twenty-one, she has applied her powerful pen to report,
unceasingly and across media platforms, on issues affecting Chicago's LGBT (Lesbian, Gay,
Bisexual, and Transgender) community. Baim is committed to protecting the rights of LGBT
individuals with a stream of hard-news journalism, as well as reporting on cultural aspects of
the community that are rarely covered elsewhere.*

*Her full-body engagement with sometimes-controversial issues has earned her abundant
accolades, including a Studs Terkel Community Media Award. Among her books are*
Out and Proud in Chicago, an Overview of the City's Gay Community *and*
Obama and the Gays: A Political Marriage. *She holds a B.A. in journalism from
Iowa's Drake University.*

My mother, Joy Darrow, and my stepfather, Steve Pratt, were *Chicago Tribune*
reporters in the '60s. My mom was frustrated at always being assigned "women's
stories," and she began forging an alternative path in 1968 by covering the
Democratic National Convention. She later worked for the *Chicago Defender* and
piggybacked on human rights trips to places like Cuba and Haiti. Her passion
was to be in the heart of chaos to document important experiences. She and my
stepdad were absolutely my role models.

I began freelancing in gay media in 1984, right out of college. There was a belief
that you couldn't make it as an openly gay journalist; it could be a career killer.
My life has not been more difficult because I'm openly gay, but I struggled with
it from a career perspective. I attempted suicide during my sophomore year at
Drake, which forced me to enter counseling. Through my journal writing, I came
out as a lesbian to a professor of mine who I knew was gay but also was married.
He responded back, assuring me that it would get better with time.

My parents had several gay friends. When I was in college, at a party, one of them
said my mom wanted him to ask me whether I was gay. I told him she should talk
to me herself. Later, in our kitchen, she asked me whether I had boyfriends. I said,
"If you don't know I'm gay by now, I don't even know what to say to you," and I
left the room abruptly.

That night was a pivot point for her. She moved toward total open acceptance and two years later helped me find my first job, at the *Gay Life* newspaper. In 1985, at twenty-two, I co-founded *Windy City Times*. Some of the reporters we worked with were still in the closet. Although alternative media began thriving in the '60s, gay media was new. We were the double underground of alternative media.

My workday usually spans sixteen hours, on and off. The drive I experience comes, in part, from seeing others struggle with drugs and alcohol when I was a teen. It created a "reverse role modeling" in me. I've always loved sports and assumed huge responsibilities in that area – running softball and soccer leagues and planning travel and game schedules. Participation in team sports teaches you everything you need to know about life – such as budgeting, learning to both win *and* lose, and negotiating all kinds of personalities.

Carrying huge responsibility has been my own choice; it works for me. Because of a commitment to documenting the gay community through reporting, I learned the business aspects of publishing primarily as a means to doing what I love – reporting. I've created my own destiny. To be successful, especially today, you need discipline, structure, and focus. In school, nobody teaches you how to get from A to Z. Your own passion and ideas are what lead to your desired outcome.

[Baim then quoted a speech she made at Valparaiso University in the mid '90s.] "What I really want is for all gays and lesbians to accept themselves. I would like for the internal homophobia to stop, for the self-destructive behavior and the suicide to end. All we seek from society is the right to live peacefully, without violence and discrimination based on our sexual orientation. Our future depends on making sure everyone is included." That statement is as true as it ever was. Although many people are totally accepting of gay people, others still hate us. Personally, I would rather have died than lived in the closet.

*Tracy Baim was interviewed at her Chicago home on the Near South Side on September 29, 2011.*

## Favorites

**BOOK**
*The Immortal Life of Henrietta Lacks* by Rebecca Skloot. As a journalist, the book is inspirational because the writer worked on it for ten years with no assignment, publisher, or outside funding. It's a great story of medical intrigue and social injustice.

**MOVIE**
*Tipping the Velvet* (2002). It's a TV miniseries set in the 1890s that depicts a lesbian love affair.

**NONPROFIT**
Crossroads Community Fund. The organization supports a wide range of grassroots groups and displays a real commitment to social justice.

**PERFORMER**
Actress Sharon Gless. She's fearless.

**QUOTATION**
"Revolution is not a one-time event."
— AUDRE LORDE, AFRICAN AMERICAN LESBIAN-FEMINIST WRITER

"*Revolution is not a one-time event.*"

Photo courtesy of Erikson Institute

# Barbara Bowman

## Co-Founder, Erikson Institute

Tireless advocate for early education strives to ensure a more equitable future for the world's less-advantaged children.

*Born into a family of privilege, Barbara Bowman was made aware from her youngest years that the advantages she experienced came with responsibilities – an obligation to enhance the lives of others, particularly in the city her prominent family called home, Chicago. Her grandfather, Robert Robinson Taylor, was a vice president of Tuskegee Institute, a private, historically black university located in Tuskegee, Alabama. (An architect, her grandfather designed the university.) Later, Bowman's father, Robert Rochon Taylor, chaired the Chicago Housing Authority. As a girl, she made her home at the Rosenwald Apartments, a building complex that her father managed, located at 47th and Michigan Avenue on Chicago's South Side. Built in 1929 to offer quality, affordable housing to African Americans, the Rosenwald met that objective for five decades before falling into disrepair.*

*She followed her mother's path by becoming a teacher, earning her bachelor's from Sarah Lawrence College in Bronxville, New York, and a master of arts from the University of Chicago. Bowman taught for sixteen years before co-founding Erikson Institute.* Erikson is one of the nation's premier graduate schools focused on child development, and it continually strives to improve the care and education of children from birth to age eight. She is the Irving B. Harris Professor of Child Development and served as Erikson's president from 1994-2001. Her résumé also includes eight years as chief early education officer for the Chicago Public Schools. Among the many accolades bestowed upon Bowman are five honorary degrees, the McGraw Prize in Education, and the Chicago Historical Society's Jane Addams Award. She is the mother of Valerie Jarrett, a key advisor to President Barack Obama.*

My sister and I were always involved in community activities because our parents and grandparents set that example. They also made certain that we were active in the life of the mind. As a young African American woman in the 1940s, I realized how truly exceptional it was that both of my parents and most of my relatives were college graduates. There was never a doubt that I would attend college. My father was a successful businessman, and he mentored recent graduates of the Tuskegee Institute who had moved north to set up entrepreneurial enterprises. My mother was immersed in church and other volunteer activities. I remember rolling bandages with her during World War II to send to troops overseas.

I graduated from Sarah Lawrence College in Bronxville, New York, in 1950 and was soon married and settled in Chicago. While working on my teaching certificate, I contacted the Chicago Board of Education to arrange an observation of a kindergarten class. I was shocked at what I saw – a teacher played the piano as she maintained a running commentary, often screaming at her large group of about fifty children. The incident was discouraging, but it provided a catalyst for me to attend graduate school at the University of Chicago and study education and work at the highly respected Lab School. When I began teaching there, at twenty-one, I was somewhat intimidated but – more importantly – immediately intrigued by the young children I came to know.

Later in my career, international educational experiences in Iran and England offered new lessons. During those periods, I became more aware of the need to help children from low-income families achieve success in school. At an orphanage in Iran, I saw children who had been deprived of the nurturing relationships that are essential to a happy life. This became a major interest for me. At that time in the U.S., few teachers were prepared to teach poor preschool children. With the launch of the Head Start Program in 1965, we began addressing the reality that poor children didn't know the same things that middle-class kids did, things that lead to school success.

We started Erikson Institute in 1966 to respond to the critical need for early childhood professionals who could staff the rapidly expanding number of programs for young children. The institute is named for Erik Erikson, a German-born American developmental psychologist and psychoanalyst. He was among the first in his field to propose that children are products of society's expectations, prejudices, and prohibitions. In addition to the critical work of training educators, we address real-world challenges through programs like the *Fussy Baby Network*. It supports parents who are struggling to care for babies who are fussy, cry excessively, or have difficulties sleeping or feeding.

We still need to accomplish a great deal to ensure that all young children are given a good start in life. I am mystified that we can't seem to obtain the financial resources needed to assist low-income youngsters – considering that *we know how to do it*. It makes much more sense to dedicate financial resources at the front end rather than to pay the price of unemployment and incarceration later.

The most important job of parents, clearly, is to build and sustain good relationships with their children. Mothers and fathers should spend time enjoying their kids and letting their children enjoy their company, too. When parents make sufficient time to do the ordinary things – such as reading or visiting the playground – strong attachments typically will develop. As long as a child feels well loved, she will sense that her parents are doing the most they can to support her best interests. When parents experience trouble getting on the same wavelength as their children, they should seek help. Early intervention makes a difference.

*Barbara Bowman was interviewed at Erikson Institute on N. LaSalle Street in Chicago on June 27, 2012. Her birthday is October 30, 1928.*

---

## Favorites

**BOOKS**
Old English mysteries written by women.

**MOVIE**
*The African Queen* (1951), directed by John Huston. It's one of many classic films that I like. Starring Humphrey Bogart and Katharine Hepburn, the 1951 adventure film is adapted from the 1935 novel of the same name by C. S. Forester.

**PLACE**
Shiraz, Iran, where my daughter was born.

**QUOTATION**
"Hang in!"

★ Child psychologist Maria Piers and social worker Lorraine Wallach are the other co-founders of Erikson Institute. Businessman and philanthropist Irving B. Harris provided financial support.

"Hang in!"

# Marca Bristo

## Disability Rights Champion

A diving accident provided her with
the most meaningful life she could (never)
have envisioned.

*Marca Bristo is a nationally and internationally acclaimed leader in the disability rights movement. She is the co-founder, president, and chief executive officer of Access Living of Metropolitan Chicago, one of the first ten centers created for independent living in the country (1980). Among many other honors, Bristo has been awarded the Distinguished Service Award of the President of the United States and the Americans with Disabilities Act Award for her role in the creation and passage of the 1990 law.*

*Today, as president of the United States International Council on Disabilities, she leads the campaign to advance the ratification of the United Nations Convention on the Rights of People with Disabilities in the U.S. Bristo holds a bachelor's degree in Sociology from Beloit College in Wisconsin and a bachelor's degree in Nursing from Rush College of Nursing, Chicago.*

At age twenty-three, I was on my way to becoming a midwife when my life was interrupted by a spinal cord accident that left me paralyzed. I was out on the pier with friends at Pratt Street Beach in Rogers Park. A dog knocked my shoes into the water, and I dove in to retrieve them. When I hit the water, everything turned black and then swirled around me. I thought I was dying. When I bobbed above the water, my friend carefully lowered himself into the water to come after me. I saw that it wasn't even as deep as his knees. Because of my nursing background, I quickly realized that something was seriously wrong. Within two weeks, it was clear I'd never walk again.

I thought I had "accepted" what had happened pretty quickly, but I was in denial about my denial. I later learned that I'd internalized all the depression. Society sends many messages that devalue you and make you feel less than equal. Coming into the Disability Rights Movement brought my old self and my new self together.

In 1977, while working as a nurse at Prentice Women's Hospital at Northwestern Memorial Hospital, I studied my patients' records and discovered that women with disabilities were rarely asked about their sexuality, which made me very angry. It was another indication of how society viewed people with disabilities as invisible. After speaking to my supervisor, I attended a conference in Berkeley, California, on the topic of sexuality, family planning, and disability.

My real transformation started then, in large part because I saw how different things were in Berkeley. There were curb cuts everywhere as well as buses with lifts, so people in wheelchairs could get around by themselves more easily. Plus, I stayed up all night talking with a woman, who also had a disability, with whom I really connected. She helped me understand that it was because of disability activism in California that things were so much different in Berkeley than they were in Chicago.

When I arrived home, I realized that I couldn't get myself to the grocery store a block and a half away because the sidewalks were inaccessible, not because I used a wheelchair. I soon joined a committee that dealt with issues of independent living – which I'd declined to do several times earlier – at the Rehabilitation Institute of Chicago. I became increasingly committed and involved with these concerns. What evolved became Access Living.

The person who has inspired me the most is my mother. She struggled with medical problems her entire life, but she remained tenacious and always looked on the bright side of her situation. Although she experienced many struggles, she did so with considerable humility, and I learned a great deal from watching her. From a disability perspective, I've learned you can go through what the world perceives to be awful medical circumstances and not only remain intact but, importantly, you can still be a force for good in the world.

If I had not experienced my accident, would I have become a social activist? Maybe I would have gotten involved with some other issue, simply because of the era in which I grew up. It's a matter of observing and listening to what is going on around you: Is there a call there for you? The Disability Movement helped me reclaim the power I lost after my accident. As a result, I've made a contribution and been part of something far larger than myself.

I've heard it said that we're on a journey to ourselves. Fortunately, I never had to search for the meaning of my life: It's always been clear to me. The circumstances of my life have given me the richest experience I could possibly imagine.

*Marca Bristo was interviewed on October 18, 2010 at Access Living in the River North neighborhood. Her birthday is June 23, 1953.*

---

## Favorites

**BOOKS**
*The Alexandria Quartet* by Lawrence Durrell. The four books present different perspectives on a single set of events and characters in Alexandria, Egypt, before and during World War II.

**PERFORMERS**
Bob Marley, Melissa Etheridge, and Bruce Springsteen. They are soulful, deep, and a little raw in talking about the human experience.

**PLACE**
Lake Michigan, which is quite ironic since this is where my journey all began.

**QUOTATION**
"Nothing about us without us."
— THE SLOGAN OF THE DISABILITY MOVEMENT

"Nothing about us without us."

# Johnpaul Cafiero

## From Police Officer to Priest

An Oz-like journey helped him redefine his calling.

*Born to the cloth – be it a law enforcement uniform or a monk's robe – Friar Johnpaul Cafiero, OFM (Order of Friars Minor), is today a Franciscan Priest of the Sacred Heart Province of Chicago/St. Louis. His church assignments have included a stint as a chaplain at the Cook County Juvenile Detention Center, where he counseled gang members in conjunction with the gang-crimes unit of the Chicago Police Department. Cafiero holds an M.A. in Counseling Psychology from Boston University. He earned his Master of Divinity from the Catholic Theological Union at the University of Chicago and Doctor of Ministry (Psychology/Theology) at the University of St. Mary of the Lake in Mundelein, Illinois. Cafiero is a chaplain for the Illinois State Police.*

As the oldest of five children of an Italian/Polish family, my life script was written very early. In Jersey City, we lived right down the street from the parish. The Dominican fathers walked the streets of our neighborhood, and the church was central to our lives. When my father and my mother fought – loudly – I would gather up my siblings inside a hula-hoop and head for the sanctuary. I always experienced a peaceful sense of mystery in that big Gothic church whose doors were never closed. It represented an escape when things were crazy at home.

While an undergraduate majoring in psychology and philosophy, I also studied at the police academy. My Uncle Charlie, who was a sheriff and a surrogate father to us, inspired my interest in law enforcement. I planned a career that would combine law enforcement and counseling. My intention was always to make the world a better place, and working with the Emergency Services Unit – using my degree in marriage and family counseling – was a great way to help people. During my time with the Jersey City Police Emergency Service Auxiliary Unit, I counseled victims at the scenes of emergencies and accidents. At the end of four years in law enforcement, my partner on the unit was shot and killed. I realized, of course, that it could have been me. The question arose, "Is this really the way I want to serve?" The event caused me to consider other ways to fulfill my calling.

When I chose to join the Franciscans, I didn't view it as a major career shift because both professions offer a vital way to be available to others and make a positive contribution. One of my assignments was Vice President of Spiritual Life and Pastoral Counseling at Hales Franciscan High School on Chicago's

South Side at 4900 S. Cottage Grove Ave. I interacted with so many young men who were sorely lacking role models, many of whom, without intervention, would become gangbangers and street warriors. I started a mentoring program featuring many motivational speakers, including a young community organizer named Barack Obama.

This wonderful chapter in my life lasted twelve years. People often ask me whether the vows of celibacy and chastity are difficult, and I say that, at times, it is lonely to be without one unique person with whom to share your life. However, at Hales, I used to joke, "I have 350 sons and they all go home when the bell rings." As a mentor, you pass on your passion, values, and essence. By your influence, you live on in others very powerfully.

A precocious kid, I asked the nuns endless questions, always looking for realistic answers. For example: "Did the snake in the Garden of Eden *really* talk to Adam and Eve? *Really*?" They'd explain that such occurrences were mysteries, and I've learned to fully embrace life's mysteries.

I love storytelling, and one of the parish missions, or spiritual retreats, I offer is based on my favorite book, *The Wizard of Oz*. I view it as a spiritual odyssey about the journey through life. Everybody can relate to it. Journeys often begin because someone is trying to escape his or her life. On Dorothy's quest, she was seeking something very different from her life in Kansas. The story contains every component a good journey requires, including difficult life lessons, like how to survive haunted forests and flying monkeys. The journey is strongly shaped by the companions who teach her so much. Take the Scarecrow: He showed Dorothy about the need to feel things and to live fully, even though he believed he had no brain. The Tin Man thought he didn't have a heart . . . but look how well he expressed emotion. I was always told in the police academy that we shouldn't express emotions. But hello! I'm Italian. I cry at Hallmark commercials.

*Johnpaul Cafiero was interviewed at his Ashland Avenue home, a friary on Chicago's North Side, on September 19, 2011. (A yellow brick road meanders through the backyard's verdant garden.) His birthday is August 2, 1954.*

---

## Favorites

**SPIRITUAL BOOK**
*Francis: The Journey and the Dream* by Friar Murray Bodo. The book is about St. Francis's transformation from a knight to a soldier of God.

**MOVIE**
*The Wizard of Oz* (1939), directed by Victor Fleming. I consider it a template for life's spiritual journey.

**POEM**
"God's Grandeur" by Jesuit priest and poet Gerard Manley Hopkins. The poem includes these lines:

"The world is charged with the grandeur of God
  It will flame out, like shining from shook foil;
  It gathers to a greatness, like the ooze of oil
  Crushed. Why do men then now not reck his rod?"

**SONG**
"Breathe." It's a contemporary hymn written by Michael Smith.

**QUOTATION**
"When you serve the least, you serve me."
        – GOSPEL OF ST. MATTHEW, CHAPTER 25

*"When you serve the least..."*

# Helen Cameron

## Co-Owner, Uncommon Ground

Growing community through her restaurants while pioneering the country's first certified-organic rooftop farm satisfies her heart's desire.

*Helen Cameron and her husband, Michael, own the restaurants Uncommon Ground, with two locations – one in Wrigleyville and one in Edgewater. The couple is recognized not only for providing exceptional food, hospitality, and live entertainment, but also for their leadership in cutting-edge environmental practices, sustainability, and urban farming. The 3,000-square-foot location at Clark Street in Wrigleyville began welcoming patrons in 1991, followed by a 4,000-square-foot venue on Devon Avenue, in Edgewater, in 2007.*

*Uncommon Ground accomplished an ambitious goal when it debuted the country's first certified-organic rooftop farm (given the stamp of approval by the Midwest Organic Services Association) in 2008. Another distinction: Uncommon Ground is among the "Greenest Restaurants in America," as certified by the Green Restaurant Association. It is a member of Slow Food, a global, grassroots organization with supporters in 150 countries worldwide that link the pleasure of good food with commitments to their communities and the environment.*

My memories of growing up west of Humboldt Park are vivid. There were strong food affinities on both sides of my family. My mom was from Cologne, Germany. When she came to the U.S. at age twenty-four, she began working at Kuhn's Delicatessen on Lincoln Avenue, and I started learning to cook, by her side, at age five. My Dad and my grandmother maintained an amazing garden that even today evokes memories of magical harvests. I recall waking up in the middle of the night to pick and eat luscious ripe tomatoes before going back to bed. European attitudes shaped my life. I learned about organic gardening and composting at an early age. From as far back as I can remember, the experience of cooking and eating with family and friends has created spiritual, joyful connections.

Spirituality plays a definite role in what we do. Our operating philosophy is that Uncommon Ground isn't just a business; it's a means for developing community. Everything is connected. When you are aligned with positive forces, success and growth directly result from those beliefs and actions. It's so important to look at what makes the most sense – for everyone involved and for the environment. We've never operated by conventional business wisdom. For example, Uncommon Ground doesn't advertise; instead, those resources are invested into food and music. We support the local arts scene by highlighting emerging musicians and artists. In 1995, singer-songwriter Jeff Buckley played at the Wrigleyville location. Ever since his death in 1997, we've held an annual benefit in his honor to benefit Chicago's Old Town School of Folk Music.

"Organic" wasn't even a factor when we opened in 1991. The precursor to that movement was a decision to buy from trusted local vendors and farmers. We always asked about the methods they used to grow or source their products. Our opening questions are always, "How can we help each other? What is the symbiosis?" Recycling and repurposing is integral to outfitting the restaurants. For example, our tables are crafted of reclaimed wood from Jackson Park. Our monthly eco-mixers, the Green Room Sessions, create a social environment for networking to develop a sustainable community of like-minded individuals.

Timing has played a role in our success. The creation of the Green City Market in 1999 was a major milestone. [Note: The mission of Green City Market is to provide a marketplace for purchasing sustainably grown food and to educate, promote, and connect farmers and local producers directly to chefs, restaurateurs, and the greater local community.]

When I first saw the rooftop at our Devon location, I immediately pictured an organic farm. Development of our farm was fundamentally complementary to our overall mission. Our second full season of operation was in 2010, and we produced 659 pounds of exceptional food, plus over forty pounds of honey from our beehives. The roof houses five thermal solar panels to heat our water. They produce 10 percent of our overall energy needs.

The person who inspires me most is my husband, Michael. We're partners in every sense of the word. Knowing there's someone who has your back – no matter what – makes everything else so much easier. Our mission is to stand as a working model for other restaurants, businesses, and homeowners to showcase what's possible within an urban environment while operating efficiently and economically.

*Helen Cameron was interviewed at Uncommon Ground in Edgewater on March 29, 2011. Her birthday is April 21, 1963.*

## Favorites

**MUSIC**
"Hallelujah," the Leonard Cohen song as performed by Jeff Buckley.

**PLACE**
Waimoku Falls in Haleakala National Park, Hawaii. A round-trip trek of five miles rewards hikers with the magnificence of this 400-foot waterfall.

**SPIRITUAL BOOK**
*Self-Enfoldment by Disciplines of Realization* by Manly P. Hall. This basic text for those seeking inner growth offers practical instructions in the philosophy of disciplined thinking and feeling, with the goal of releasing and developing inward perceptions.

**QUOTATION**
"Never, never, never give up."
– WINSTON CHURCHILL, FORMER PRIME MINISTER OF THE UNITED KINGDOM

"*Never, never, never give up.*"

# Gloria Castillo

## CEO, Chicago United

Politically shaped by the women's movement, she works to create a more equitable Chicago for people of all colors.

*After her mother, Mona, crashed through the proverbial "glass ceiling" to become a business owner when Gloria Castillo was a teenager, Gloria responded by immersing herself in the nascent Chicago Chapter of the National Organization for Women (NOW) in 1972. The camaraderie and heady empowerment she experienced there galvanized her to seek other opportunities to help balance the scales of opportunity for less-fortunate Chicagoans. After more than twenty years as a business executive and successful business owner, Castillo became involved with Chicago United.*

*A historic organization, Chicago United advocates multiracial leadership in business and equal access to opportunities in executive level management, corporate board governance, and supplier diversity. Born of the tumult of the 1960s, Chicago United commits itself to the development of key relationships across racial groups.*

*Castillo is widely credited with revitalizing the organization since she became president in 2003. Her numerous awards include Minority Small Business Champion of the Year (from the Small Business Administration) and the Corporate Social Responsibility Award from the Mexican American Legal Defense and Educational Fund (MALDEF), a national nonprofit civil rights organization that protects the rights of Latinos in the U.S.*

Growing up in Lakeview, our neighbors were German and Irish. We were the first Latinos on the block. As a family, we were not sidetracked by barriers. My mom spent her childhood in a largely Jewish neighborhood and was comfortable among people of different ethnicities. My dad, Anastacio, relocated from San Antonio, Texas. Although people may not realize it, in the late '40s many Chicago restaurants had signs in the window that warned, "No coloreds, and no Mexicans." There were also barriers in employment. When he applied using his given name, Anastacio Castillo, my dad didn't get hired. But when he applied under his nickname, "Tom," he found a job quickly.

For me, the challenges were slightly different. I attended a Catholic high school, The Immaculata. The school, now closed, was predominantly Irish and the nuns were strongly oriented towards the dominant group. I was actively discouraged from applying to the school of my choice, Northwestern University – even though I was in the top 10 percent of my class. I briefly attended Mundelein College and later pursued my degree and graduated from University of California at Santa Barbara. U.C. Santa Barbara was unlike any of my previous educational experiences. I majored in political science and absolutely came alive.

My activity with the women's movement provided the inspiration to study political science. Looking back on that experience, the accomplishment of which I am most proud is my contribution to changing the credit laws that discriminated against women. When I became involved with the issue in 1973, women could only obtain credit through their husbands or fathers – not independently. Although I was just nineteen years old, I spent every minute I could working alongside other women to change the law. Our "actions," as we called these protests, targeted Sears, a retail behemoth back then. When staging the action here in Chicago, we coordinated with NOW chapters around the country so they could also protest publicly. Although we had little money and no official clout, our strengths were our great passion, intellectual resources, endless energy, and strategy for success.

In October 1974, the Equal Credit Opportunity Act was passed. Forcing that change was a victory and a personal turning point for me. I learned that monumental shifts can be accomplished when people of like mind and passion work together.

At the time that Chicago United was created, the need for change was enormous. That was in 1968, right after the fires raged on Chicago's West Side in the wake of Dr. King's assassination. In fact, some of our organizational founders saw the flames burning – not far from their own high-rise offices in the Loop. Collectively, they said, "We must take responsibility for Chicago's future, and that means building relationships in the neighborhoods that are burning right now." Chicago United began with the commitment of thirteen CEOs of prominent companies, including ComEd, Jewel-Osco, First National Bank of Chicago, and Inland Steel.

Before I became president of Chicago United, the organization had fallen behind and had lost some credibility. Some of our members were weary of hearing about our plans for change. When I told Scott Smith, then publisher of the *Chicago Tribune,* about my ideas, he said, "That's nice. *Prove it.*" I returned to my office, typed and printed out his words, and placed them in a frame that remains on my desk today.

*Gloria Castillo was interviewed in her Randolph Street office on March 23, 2012. Her birthday is September 3, 1954.*

## Favorites

**AUTHOR**
Pearl S. Buck. In my youth, her writing had a huge impact on me. I was moved by many of her main characters – strong women that displayed great humanity.

**MOVIE**
*West Side Story* (1961), directed by Jerome Robbins and Robert Wise. It was the first film I ever saw in which Latinos played prominent roles.

**PLACE**
Lincoln Park Zoo. It's always the same, but animal behaviors make it different every time you visit.

**QUOTATION**
"Never doubt that a small group of thoughtful, committed citizens can change the world. Indeed, it's the only thing that ever has."
– MARGARET MEAD, AMERICAN ANTHROPOLOGIST

"*a small group...can change the world.*"

# Danny Davis

## Congressman, U.S. House of Representatives

This son of sharecroppers lives an activist's version of the American dream.

*Danny K. Davis was elected to the House of Representatives, representing the 7th Congressional District of Illinois, in January 1997. His political résumé was developed initially as the first independent, non-Machine candidate to be elected to the Chicago City Council from Chicago's West Side as alderman of the 29th Ward. It was a notable achievement; white ward bosses had long controlled African American aldermen. Davis was later elected to the office of Cook County Commissioner (1990-94). In 1991, he lost his bid to become mayor of Chicago. (If the outcome had been different, Davis would have become the city's second African American mayor, following in the footsteps of friend and mentor Mayor Harold Washington). As a congressional representative, Davis particularly champions issues related to criminal justice reform, poverty, education, and healthcare access.*

*Davis's comfortable, casual office is located on West Arthington Street in Chicago. When he arrived for our meeting, he was wearing a Cubs jacket and a baseball cap. He is that refreshing rarity – a politician with absolutely no pretension. An office crowded with cardboard file boxes and a desk piled high with papers, countless awards, and memorabilia evidences this poetry-quoting congressman's hands-on approach. Ever accessible to his constituents, Davis maintains weekly office hours and hosts many town meetings – always has. He came to politics through a most natural route – as a community organizer, healthcare administrator, educator, and civil rights advocate.*

*A natural storyteller, Davis regales visitors with anecdotes about his parents, Hezekiah "H.D." Davis and Mazzie Lee Glass Davis, who attended school through the fourth and eighth grades, respectively. He fondly recalls how very smart his parents were, despite the lack of much formal education. Thanks to them, a small scholarship, and his own super work ethic, Danny Davis graduated from Arkansas AM&N College (later the University of Arkansas-Pine Bluff). He earned both a master's and a doctorate from, respectively, Chicago State University and the Union Institute, Cincinnati, Ohio.*

The sign at the "city limits" of Parkdale, Arkansas, always read "Population: 267." If you included the families that lived outside of town on farms like ours, that number increased to about 500. I started school in a one-room schoolhouse. We lived five or six miles away, and I walked there every day with my three older sisters. [He is one of ten children, total, of the same father, who had two different wives.] Growing up on a farm was fun. The idea was, "every tub sits on its own bottom." In other words, each person contributed. We attended school five months of the year so we could help on the farm when needed. I began chopping and picking cotton at age six. The only difference between my bag and an adult's bag was that mine was shorter.

I read a lot of biographies and autobiographies as a kid, although we didn't have many books. Because of my mom, I became a great Abraham Lincoln fan. I began learning about Black history and becoming more aware of Black culture through the KYB (Know Your Bible) Club at church. Besides learning about religion [at this point, he stops to recite the names of the books of the Bible], we became comfortable with etiquette and how to be social. We were taught not to be embarrassed because we didn't have money to take the girls we liked to the movies. Instead, I realized that I could walk down the road, pick some wildflowers, take her for a walk and quote poetry – maybe some Shakespeare: "Shall I compare thee to a summer's day? Thou art more lovely and more temperate. Rough winds do shake the darling buds of May, And summer's lease hath all too short a date."

Through my parents and my community, I always heard about this business of hope, this business of possibility. The spirit was so strong around us. Sometimes you'd get mad when you encountered a difficult situation, like somebody stealing from you or someone calling you a nigger. But because of our positive surroundings, we'd always overcome it.

After graduating from college with a degree in education in 1961, I headed for Chicago with hopes of becoming a history teacher. I began teaching in 1962 at Magellan Educational and Vocational Center, a special school for underachievers in North Lawndale. Community development work quickly intrigued me, which led me to politics.

After traveling all over the country doing community organizing with many kinds of groups and organizations that wanted to be empowered, I'd learned the important lesson that while advocates can work for change, *elected officials make decisions*. I realized that being a legislator would be the most effective way to help bring about the changes that weren't happening as fast as I thought they could, or should, be. But, I've learned so much about how change *actually* happens. I still love to listen to Sam Cooke's 1963 classic, "A Change Is Gonna Come." It is often more covert than overt. Change is more evolution than revolution. Savvy veterans know you can't pinpoint what triggers a particular change at a particular point in time. For example, what finally caused so many people in America to think, as they do now, that same-sex marriage should be legalized?

My proudest accomplishment? Helping people understand that change can happen. All things are possible if you believe they are. I'd just as soon believe I can fly as believe that I can't.

*Danny Davis was interviewed at his Near West Side office on January 9, 2013. His birthday is September 6, 1941.*

---

## Favorites

**BOOK**
The Bible. It contains so much wisdom.

**MOVIE**
*The Butler* (2013), directed by Lee Daniels. The film is inspired by the experiences of Eugene Allen, the distinguished African American butler who served eight U.S. presidents in the White House.

**PLACE**
My living room. It's so peaceful.

**POEM**
"Invictus" by William Ernest Henley. Here are the closing lines:

"I am the master of my fate,
 I am the captain of my soul."

**QUOTATION**
"Power concedes nothing without a demand. It never did and it never will."
– FREDERICK DOUGLASS, AFRICAN AMERICAN SOCIAL REFORMER, ORATOR, WRITER, AND STATESMAN

"*Power concedes nothing without a demand.*"

# Richard Dent

## NFL Hall of Famer and Former Chicago Bear

Emerging from a hardscrabble childhood, he parlayed a roster of hardships into athletic excellence.

*Coming of age as the sixth of nine children in a financially strapped family, Richard Dent early on mastered independence, discipline, and self-sufficiency – survival skills that served him well in later pursuit of football gold. His ascent to a 1985 Chicago Bears Super Bowl victory and a 2011 Hall of Fame election is best characterized as an uphill climb marked by obstacles, remarkable mentors, and a sheer tenacity matched only by his own brute strength. (In his tenure with the Chicago Bears, the six-feet-five-inch tall defensive leader weighed in at 265 pounds.)*

*The Chicago Bears chose Dent in the eighth round of the 1983 draft. Only two years later, he was celebrated as the Bears' all-time leader in quarterback sacks (which occur when the quarterback is tackled behind the line of scrimmage). "The Sack Man" also suited up for the San Francisco 49ers, the Indianapolis Colts, and the Philadelphia Eagles. He did two stints with the Chicago Bears, for a total of twelve years.*

*Dent is the founder of RLD Resources, a Chicago-based company specializing in energy and telecommunication issues. He created the Make a Dent Foundation in honor of his mother, Mary, to provide scholarships for students pursuing careers in sports management at Columbia College, Chicago, among other initiatives. His book* Blood, Sweat & Bears: Putting a "Dent" in the Game I Love, *was published in 2012.*

Most of the boys in my family were "daddy's boys," always seeking my father's attention, so I became a "mama's boy" instead. My mother was like Aibileen Clark, the African American servant in the movie *The Help*. She raised other people's kids while doing their cooking and cleaning. On Tuesdays and Thursdays, she prepared food at church. My mother did everything for everybody; that's how I became connected to the idea of servicing people, which I do today through my business and my foundation. My mom was my role model – the most loving, giving, and spiritual person I've ever known.

From childhood, I've been an underdog who worked diligently to develop inner motivation. Even as a chubby kid with dental problems and a learning disability, I always pushed onward. When there's a wall in front of me, I find a way to get over it and continue moving forward.

As a kid, I was surrounded by trouble but worked hard to keep myself out of it. Three of my four brothers spent time in prison, and one is still incarcerated today. Wanting something better for myself, I began earning money by age ten. Since I was a big kid, it was easy for me to get jobs.

My childhood dream was to become a professional athlete, but I couldn't play on a team until my junior year in high school because I was always working. Fortunately, one day my friend Scott Dean and I dared each other to try out for the team. He told me, "You've already proved you can support yourself – if you have to – by doing physical labor. Why not pursue your dreams *now*, while you have the opportunity?" He did me a huge favor.

I wasn't heavily recruited out of high school, but my coach, William Lester, was intent upon getting me a scholarship to Tennessee State, where several of my teammates were headed. He knew how badly I wanted to leave Atlanta and start a life somewhere else. When I arrived with Coach Lester, he simply told Joe Gilliam, the legendary coach of Tennessee State, that I was part of a package deal.

Coach Gilliam allowed me to shine, and that's what effective leaders do. After he saw how I continually "polished the stone" that was my playing ability – making it sparkle more and more in practice – he quickly realized how much I could bring to the team. He was a wise man, too. Coach Gilliam understood people. If you did something wrong, he didn't push you away. Instead, he drew you closer to him.

Clearly, an individual's achievements are a direct reflection of the amount of work he's willing to invest in his goals. The head coach at Tennessee State, John Merritt, used to say, "The hay is in the barn," meaning that we, as players, needed to work out consistently and hard to prepare ourselves for our weekly game. If you had been putting hay in the barn all week, you were far more likely to go out to the field on game day and finish off the job.

By the time I was halfway through college, I became convinced I could make it in the NFL. I concentrated a great deal on who made it there and who didn't – and why. When you're focused on a goal, you must step outside of yourself to envision what you need to do to reach your objective. If you don't know where you're going, how can you expect to be successful?

When the Bears drafted me, my character had already been molded and shaped. Unfortunately, I never received the recognition I deserved on the team. The fans loved me, but the organization didn't. Being named MVP of Super Bowl XX was an honor, but the ultimate highlight of my football career was my 2011 election to the Pro Football Hall of Fame after many previous nominations. The honor embraces my entire career and acknowledges contributions over fifteen seasons in the NFL.

*Richard Dent was interviewed at the offices of RLD Resources on Michigan Avenue in Chicago on March 4, 2013. His birthday is December 13, 1960.*

## Favorites

**BOOK**
*I Have a Dream: Writings and Speeches that Changed the World* by Martin Luther King, Jr.

**MOVIE**
*Brian's Song* (1971), directed by Buzz Kulik. It personifies what teamwork is all about and illustrates how some of your teammates become like family members.

**PLACE**
Harry Caray's Tavern on Navy Pier. It's a great, comfortable spot to relax.

**QUOTATION**
"There are three classes of people: those who see; those who see when they are shown; and those who do not see."
– LEONARDO DA VINCI, LEADING FIGURE OF THE ITALIAN RENAISSANCE

"*There are three classes of people...*"

# Richard Driehaus

## Financier and Philanthropist

Even as a child, this quintessential self-made man never doubted he would determine his own destiny.

*Although the two neighborhoods are only several miles apart in distance, financier Richard H. Driehaus has voyaged light years from his childhood in Brainerd, on Chicago's Southwest Side, to the gilded gates of Chicago's Gold Coast. Born of middle-class parents, Driehaus believes his early economic hardships catapulted him to the legendary success he is celebrated for today. In 1982, he founded Driehaus Capital Management LLC, a privately held, Chicago-based investment advisory firm that manages approximately $8 billion in assets (as of September 2012). An ardent "Blue Demon," he earned his bachelor's degree and an MBA from DePaul University. Only a few contribute as openhandedly as Driehaus does. Through the efforts of the Richard H. Driehaus Foundation and the Richard H. Driehaus Charitable Lead Trust, as well as through his personal wealth, he champions an array of programs to advance architecture, community initiatives, education, investigative reporting, the performing arts, and more.*

When I was ten, my father purchased a piece of land in Beverly. It was a better neighborhood, with good schools, that was much nicer than the neighborhood where we then lived in a bungalow. An architect had already been hired to build our new home, an English Tudor. I was excited about the move to a better area. Then I overheard kitchen-table conversations between my parents. My mom said we couldn't afford to build the house. This didn't make any sense to me, because my dad was a mechanical engineer who worked very hard.

I remember thinking to myself that I would *never* pursue any business venture that would not reward me generously based on my own merits.

At age eleven, I started collecting coins and reading *Coin World*. I learned which coins dealers were buying and selling, and I paid attention to what the spreads were on these in-demand coins. I used the $20 a month I earned as a newspaper boy to buy and sell semi-rare coins to dealers, which was the early start of my experience as a trader.

The first time I came across the New York Stock Exchange listings in the newspaper, at age twelve, I was intrigued. My mom directed me to my Uncle Ade, who knew the stock market. He educated me about the stocks he liked and explained the basic concept of dividends. Before I began to invest, my mom offered this great advice: "Before you invest, you have to investigate." My early reading included columns by two highly respected syndicated financial columnists. When I bought a stock they both recommended and it didn't do well, I couldn't believe it!

I then headed to the Chicago Public Library to pour through *Forbes, Fortune,* and *The Wall Street Journal*. Research showed the importance of earnings growth, so I became interested in faster-growing companies.

The motivation to make money through the markets was spurred by wanting to avoid what my father experienced. Although he had twenty-four patents and worked for a good company, it was in a declining industry with limited room for salary growth and advancement. When I discovered the markets, I discovered a way out. I knew I'd found a way to be paid based on my own hard work and performance – with unlimited potential. My parents were my role models: my dad for his diligence and desire to make a better life for us, and my mom for her own hard work. When my father had a major heart attack in the early 1950s, she supported three kids on her own.

From a young age, the School Sisters of Notre Dame have been a huge influence. Their directive that "You are responsible for your own actions" meant only I could determine my destiny. Through my life as a Catholic, I've learned that it's also my responsibility to give back. My advice: Strive to be successful in this area of your life, too. As Sir Winston Churchill said, "We make a living by what we get, but we make a life by what we give."

I've had wonderful mentors and supporters throughout my life, although I know I am described as a self-made man. I decided on a course of action early in life and worked very, very hard to make it a reality. Remember what Henry Ford said: "Whether you think you can, or you think you can't – you're right."

*Richard Driehaus was interviewed on September 22, 2011, at his company headquarters, located in the Ransom R. Cable House in the River North neighborhood. Designated a Chicago landmark in 1991, the home was built for Ransom Cable, president of the Chicago, Rock Island and Pacific Railroad. Richard Driehaus's birthday is July 27, 1942.*

---

## Favorites

**BOOK**
*How to Make Money in Stocks: A Winning System in Good Times or Bad* by William O'Neil.

**MOVIE**
*The Wizard of Oz* (1939), directed by Victor Fleming. My biggest account came from Kansas, and I have a sister named Dorothy.

**PLACE**
Lincoln Park's Alfred Caldwell Lily Pond. It's an example of Prairie School landscape architecture designed by Alfred Caldwell that is located at 125 W. Fullerton Parkway. Listed on the National Register of Historic Places, the pond is designated a National Historic Landmark.

**QUOTATION**
"Architecture, of all of the arts, is the one which acts most slowly, but most surely, on the soul."
— ERNEST DIMNET, FRENCH PRIEST AND WRITER

"Architecture, of all the arts..."

Photo by Jon Randolph

# Stuart Dybek

## Short Story Maestro

At the pinnacle of writers identified with Chicago, he draws upon a childhood that shimmered with immigrant life.

*Born into a live-out-loud community that practically dared him not to become a writer, Stuart Dybek is a natural-born storyteller with an endless collection of colorful, poetically recounted, and fond remembrances of the Pilsen and Little Village neighborhoods in which he grew up. When he was born in 1942, these areas were the domain of the Czech/Slavic population – along with Croats, Austrians, Slovenes, Poles, and other Eastern European groups – that had dominated the neighborhood, three miles south of the Chicago Loop, since the late 1800s.*

*Dybek's full-length published works include* Childhood and Other Neighborhoods, I Sailed with Magellan, *and* The Coast of Chicago, *a 2004 "One Book One Chicago"★ selection. Acclaimed as both a poet and short story master, he is the recipient of numerous literary honors. In 2007, Dybek joined the ranks of MacArthur Fellows, a distinction based on creativity, originality, and the potential to make important contributions in the future. He is the Distinguished Writer in Residence at Northwestern University and an adjunct professor of English at Western Michigan University, where he taught for nearly thirty years. Dybek earned an MFA from the Iowa Writers Workshop at the University of Iowa and holds a master's in literature from Chicago's Loyola University. His latest story collections, due in spring 2014, are* Ecstatic Cahoots *and* Paper Lantern.

I grew up in Pilsen among a large and extended family. My first home was on 18th Street off of Blue Island, and my Polish grandmother lived just a block away. We later moved to Little Village, which then was known by its postal code, Zone 8.

Mine was a pious family, and I was hugely religious as a kid. The Catholic Church plays an important role in many of my stories. I was originally drawn to words and writing through bible stories, the lives of the saints, the beauty of the psalms, and even the gory images presented in religious literature. Although I became a nonbeliever in high school, religion still fascinates me because it provides us with our original language for the awe and mystery of being human. I don't single out Catholicism; I hold strong reservations about *all* religions.

When the Hispanic migration to Chicago became evident in the mid-1950s, it seemed to me like rather a beautiful transition. I'm not sure whether Latinos would agree with my sanguine assessment, however. Pilsen evolved from a port of entry for Eastern Europeans to a port of entry for Latinos. Initially, a sense of integration existed. But as the racial and ethnic balance continued shifting, prejudice and tension surfaced in the early '60s. You could see the changes on Cermak Road: Long a destination for kraut and kielbasa, it suddenly was abundant with little taco places and Mexican grocery stores. Clearly, it made sense for Hispanics to settle in Pilsen and Little Village. The churches and bars were already established, and there's a huge overlap between Polish and Mexican values. For example, both are virgin-worshipping cultures.

Across ethnic groups, there was a strong sense of people trying to eke out a living in the middle of an industrial neighborhood. As kids, we learned how to transform the machines and edifices that surrounded us – huge coal-spewing chimneys and railroad bridges and viaducts – into our jungle gyms. We rode the slow-moving trains that passed by, grabbing the ladders on the sides of the boxcars and letting that force pull us up . . . then we'd hang on for dear life.

From the time I was very young, I spent a large amount of time with my grandmother, whom we called Busha. She offered a powerful love that was without judgment or criticism. Because Busha spoke very little English and I spoke only "pidgin" Polish, we developed a special way of emoting. Much of our communication came from sharing activities, many of them food-related. For example, we'd spend an afternoon picking Fairy Ring mushrooms and then making them into necklaces. In the process, we'd remove the caps, hang them to dry, and then add them to *kapusta* [sauerkraut] for a beautiful flavor.

My relationship with Busha and the extended immigrant family that I grew up in left a lasting impression on me that is reflected in my writing. It was the immigrant, ethnic aspects of the U.S. that seemed most vital to me and that most engaged my imagination as a child, and that sense persists. I grew up in an Eastern European neighborhood that was turning Hispanic. In my formative years, my early allegiance was to a specific ethnic group, but that changed as I grew older into a fascination with ethnic culture in general.

My early life was ideal for someone who would grow up to become a writer. Back then, people told endless stories as they gathered on street corners to socialize while drinking big glass bottles of beer. By the time I was thirteen years old, I'd seen every kind of human being I would encounter for the rest of my life, not just in terms of ethnicity, but also different psychological types.

I'm known as a Chicago writer, though I never saw myself that way. My advice to aspiring writers: Discover what kind of writer you want to be. There's more to it than learning your craft; you must explore who you are, your identity. You must want it very much, because most "literary" writers can't earn a living simply by writing. You've got to keep writing no matter what it takes, and it *will* cost you something.

*Stuart Dybek was interviewed at his Evanston residence on November 12, 2012. His birthday is April 10, 1942.*

## Favorites

**BOOKS**
*Cuttlefish Bones* by Eugenio Montale, *The Complete Short Stories of Ernest Hemingway,* and *Winesburg, Ohio* by Sherwood Anderson. (These are just a few among many beloved titles.)

**MOVIE**
*Blade Runner* (1982), directed by Ridley Scott. I love the visionary aspect of dystopia that combines with a detective-style romance to create something that is more than the sum of its parts.

**MUSIC**
Authentic klezmer music; the best is heard in Krakow.

**PLAY**
*The Tempest.* Shakespeare never fails to move me to tears, but especially when Prospero says goodbye to his spirits.

**QUOTATION**
"Chance favors a prepared mind."
– LOUIS PASTEUR, FRENCH CHEMIST AND MICROBIOLOGIST

★ According to the Chicago Public Library Foundation, "One Book, One Chicago" is an annual, citywide book club aimed at creating a community of readers. The Chicago Public Library offers a variety of free public programming such as book discussions, author series, performances, art exhibits, and films centered around the book selection.

"*Chance favors a prepared mind.*"

James Schnepf Photography

# Fritzie Fritzshall

Holocaust Survivor and President, Illinois Holocaust Museum & Education Center

"Lessons from the Holocaust are relevant to each of us today," she emphasizes.

*At eighty years of age at our meeting in June 2012, Fritzie Fritzshall (Frieda) talks like a woman with her life's work still ahead. Her days abound with critical assignments, including those that tackle genocide in Darfur and the damage wrought by bullying. Like a human alarm system, she leads the Illinois Holocaust Museum & Education Center in advancing its mission: to preserve the legacy of the Holocaust by honoring the memories of those who were murdered and by teaching universal lessons that combat hatred, prejudice, and indifference. With its unadorned, dark walls and sharp angles, the section of the building's exterior that one sees upon entering the parking lot of the Skokie structure is arresting. Most dramatically, the museum houses an authentic early twentieth-century German railcar, a boxcar of the type used to transport millions of Jews to their deaths during World War II.*

*The museum evolved from the commitment of the Holocaust Memorial Foundation of Illinois, whose tagline is "Fighting hate since 1981." The organization burst onto the scene when neo-Nazis threatened to march in Skokie, a northern Chicago suburb that is home to one of the country's largest populations of Holocaust survivors. (After much legal wrangling, an agreement was reached that relocated the march to downtown Chicago.) The museum can serve more than 250,000 visitors a year, reaching a significant portion of the nearly 2.5 million Illinois schoolchildren.*

*Except for her father, all of Fritzie Fritzshall's closest relatives died at Auschwitz. After the war ended, she was reunited with her father and moved to Chicago.*

I have wonderful memories of growing up in my small town of Klucharki, Czechoslovakia, but my childhood ended abruptly at thirteen when my village was occupied. When I went to school one morning, my teacher put up his hand to stop me as I tried to enter, telling me that Jewish children could no longer attend classes. Only a week before, this same teacher had taken a white handkerchief from his pocket and gently removed a smudge from my face. Of course, I could not answer the question: What had changed?

When I arrived home, my mother was sitting by our wood-burning stove with my two younger brothers, Elia and Mendel, in her lap. With tears in her eyes, she told us our lives would be different from now on, that the Germans now occupied our town and we needed to obey all the rules so we would not be punished. Looking back, we thought we lived in a community where our neighbors and friends would protect us, but that wasn't so. Little by little, our non-Jewish neighbors had begun stealing things from us. Their behavior was deemed acceptable because we were Jews.

Only weeks later, my family – including my grandparents, my mother, my brothers, and I – were told we were being "relocated." My father was in the U.S., completing the paperwork necessary to bring us over. Soldiers with guns pointed at us told us to pack our things, including warm clothes. People need to know that in my community, we Jews didn't know anything about the existence of concentration camps. We'd heard the words "final solution," but we didn't understand what that meant.

After living in a ghetto for a short time, one day my family members, along with many other Jews, were pushed into a standing-room-only boxcar. My mother kept telling us to stay together, but little did we know we were going to a place where families were ripped apart. Being in this boxcar was the start of breaking down our dignity. Nobody told us where we were going, and there was just one bucket in the car, which we were forced to use as a common toilet.

I survived because so many people helped me along the way, including strangers. When our train arrived at the Auschwitz-Birkenau death camp, a prisoner whose job it was to get people off the train as quickly as possible told me to lie about my age. I was thirteen, but he said to tell them I was fifteen so that, instead of being killed, I would be put to work. I was quickly separated from my mother and told that I would never see her again – and I didn't. I was, however, reunited with an aunt of mine, Bella, who helped save my life. She sacrificed her own meager food rations, offering them to other women prisoners so they would allow me to sleep in their crowded bunk bed. Every night, she held me and assured me that "tomorrow will be better."

One day, while at the door of the gas chamber, I was suddenly pulled out of line at the last second and sent to work at a factory instead. Later, when I was confined with 599 other female prisoners, they regularly gave me their crumbs of bread. Because I was the youngest, they hoped I would live to share the stories of the atrocities. I promised that I would tell the world of these horrors, but I didn't speak out for decades – not until my son convinced me to share my voice in the 1990s.

The museum has a "Power of One" campaign that emphasizes each of us has the power and responsibility to speak up for what is right. Every one of us can make a difference.

*Fritzie Fritzshall was interviewed at the museum on June 29, 2012. Her birthday is August 21, 1931.*

---

## Favorites

**BOOK**

*Unbroken: A World War II Story of Survival, Resilience, and Redemption* by Laura Hillenbrand. My husband, a U.S. Marine, was among the prisoners captured by the Japanese; this story touched me greatly on a personal level.

**PLACE**

My home in the Chicago suburbs. Family members, friends, flowers, and sunshine surround me there.

**QUOTATION**

"When you save one life, it is as if you saved the entire world."
– THE TALMUD, THE CENTRAL TEXT OF RABBINIC JUDAISM

66 *When you save one life...* 99

Photo by Stephen Hamilton

# Gale Gand

## Award-Winning Pastry Chef

Taking the cake with her *joie de vivre,* she cherry-picks culinary challenges that engage her creative entrepreneurship.

*Gale Gand, as the saying goes, is small but mighty. Petite she may be – all of five feet tall – but the Deerfield native is every inch the powerhouse. ("I make sure I never come off as little.") The former host of the Food Network's "Sweet Dreams," Gand was a partner in Trio, the groundbreaking Evanston restaurant that she created in 1994 with former husband and culinary colleague Rick Tramonto, along with another partner. (Note: Trio closed in 2006.) In 1999, Gand and Tramonto teamed up with Rich Melman to debut the four-star, five-diamond Tru, which remains one of the country's culinary gems as well as a crown jewel of the restaurant behemoth that is Lettuce Entertain You Enterprises. The author of eight cookbooks, Gand's equals among pastry chefs are very few. The late Chicago Sun-Times restaurant critic Pat Bruno extolled her as "one of the best pastry chefs in the world."*

*Gand has rewarded many a sweet tooth with her handiworks – from toasted coconut risotto with pecans to a famed "Chockablock" chocolate cake with warm caramel – in locales including Chicago, New York City, London, and Paris. Playful, passionate, and down to earth, she's equally at ease fashioning caramel apple pie pops during a TV appearance or teaching master classes at Elawa Farm in north suburban Lake Forest. Gand has cooked toque to toque with Julia Child and judged fledgling pastry chefs on TV's "Top Chef: Just Desserts." She graduated from the Rochester Institute of Technology with a BFA in metalsmithing. Later, she explored the culinary arena through studies at La Varenne in Paris.*

I am who I am because of both of my parents. My mother, Myrna, with her Jewish Hungarian roots, baked wonderfully. She made these incredible lattice-topped cherry pies. I loved cooking with her, but because of my dyslexia, I couldn't exactly follow the recipes. She'd say, with enthusiasm, "Oh, look, honey, you invented something new!" Mom possessed an open mind, a playful nature, and a lack of boundaries – just like me [laughs].

My father, Bob, was a white-collar guy with a traditional sales job who was also a natural entrepreneur. When I was six, he started a music school in our home, and it just kept growing. He came home one day when I was ten years old and announced, "Honey, I quit my job today." The music store he built in Deerfield, The Village Music Store, still operates after fifty years. My dad taught me so many lessons about discipline, creativity, self-confidence, and the courage required to change course and start something unexpected. Our family possesses a gift we describe as the Gand success gene. Somehow, things always work out for us. I've learned not to question it; instead, I just let go and trust. I'm rather fearless.

Needing to earn money in college, I worked as a server at a vegetarian restaurant. When one of the line cooks didn't show up one night, the owner asked me if I knew how to cook. When I said "No," she threw me an apron with the reply, "Well, you do now!" After five seconds of abject terror, I was overcome with a strange sense of calm. It was as if I was speaking a language that I didn't remember learning. At night's end, I was elated. I knew I'd discovered my future career. Because I'd learned from my father that it was fine to diverge from my original plan – to be an artist – I moved forward quickly.

When I'm cooking, I feel like I'm dancing. I love the combination of the skills and feelings it encompasses. I enjoy the physicality of it all. Cooking is an art form that nourishes others and embraces all the senses, while providing entertainment and the opportunity to perform.

My mentors were few, but I do recall when Julia Child asked me, "Dearie, where were you trained?" When I confided that I was self-taught, she advised, "Don't ever tell anyone that you were self-taught; rather, say you learned 'in the field.'" When Julia then asked my former husband, Rick Tramonto, where *he'd* attended culinary school, he replied that he, too, was self-taught. Julia whacked him in the arm and said, "What did I just say about that?" [laughs].

Early work experiences helped prepare me for success. I filed my first income tax at age seven or eight, based on the money I earned playing music with my dad and modeling. As a teenager, I was hired to set diamonds in a Highland Park jewelry store. Many chefs fail because they don't understand the business part of running a restaurant. Some chefs don't even know how to read a profit and loss statement. Fortunately, I developed key financial skills at an early age by working as a bookkeeper in my father's music store. I also benefit from adopting a wait-and-see attitude. I learned this philosophy from my mom: "It will all work out in the end; it always does, and worrying doesn't help, so don't do it."

I never take no for an answer. My husband, Jimmy, jokes that I think the rules don't apply to me – as in "No parking here . . . except for Gale Gand." That may be true, but I don't take advantage of the gift that is my good fortune.

*Gale Gand was interviewed in the kitchen at Elawa Farm in Lake Forest on October 18, 2012. Her birthday is November 21, 1956.*

---

## Favorites

**BOOK**

*At Home: A Short History of Private Life* by Bill Bryson. A recent favorite, the book "takes us on a room-by-room tour through his own house, using each room as a jumping off point into the vast history of the domestic artifacts we take for granted," according to the author's website.

**MOVIE**

*Shakespeare in Love* (1998), directed by John Madden. It pushed me to pursue something better for myself in my personal life.

**PLACE**

The South of France. I love its cultural attitudes and its love of food and life itself.

**QUOTATION**

"I shall have poetry in my life. And adventure. And love, love, above all . . . unbiddable, ungovernable, like a riot in the heart and nothing to be done."
– TOM STOPPARD, PLAYWRIGHT, "SHAKESPEARE IN LOVE"

"And love, love, above all..."

# Vered Hankin

## Storyteller and Meditation Teacher

Disparate as they appear to be, her two passions both help individuals become more connected to their inner lives.

*Named by* Jewish Week *as "the leading storyteller of her generation," Vered Hankin is happily impossible to categorize. She is also a psychologist, author, and meditation teacher, having trained extensively in Jon Kabat Zinn's Mindfulness Based Stress Reduction (MBSR) method at the University of Massachusetts's Center for Mindfulness. Hankin received a Bachelor of Arts from the University of Kansas, where she focused on religion and women's studies. Her Ph.D. in clinical psychology is from the City University of New York, where she wrote her dissertation on mindfulness for couples facing chronic illness. Hankin is the founder and president of MBSR Chicago. She continues her research on MBSR for chronic illness at Northwestern University's Feinberg School of Medicine and Rush University Hospital. Hankin recently co-authored two books:* Talking Treasures: Stories to Help Build Emotional Intelligence and Resilience in Young Children *and* In the Beginning: Biblical Sparks for a Child's Week. *"Vered Hankin is a storytelling marvel and a true wizard when it comes to understanding the emotional lives of children," says author Thane Rosenbaum.*

Being born and growing up in Jerusalem until the age of ten was a joyous experience. There was a sense of community that embraced singing, warmth, and togetherness; I never felt alone. Although my family was not technically observant, we lived from holiday to holiday; that cycle of celebration shaped our lives. Everything was built on telling stories, and these stories shaped who I was and how I understood my place in the world, even as a young child. At age five, I began to act out plays, including taking on other voices and changing characters, for my little sister.

My spirituality emerged when I was very young. I recall instituting a dialogue with God as a preschooler, when I walked to school by myself. I remember talking to God, in my little girl way, and enjoying that time alone. I developed a relationship with God, in part, because I had time to myself. Today's kids are so overscheduled that they don't have much opportunity to think, or just to *be*.

By age eight, I began to whisper the Sh'ma, the Jewish listening/hearing prayer that means, approximately, that there is only one God. It's the core of the Jewish faith, and you whisper it, reciting it with your hands over your eyes. The prayer turned out to be, in a way, my first meditation experience.

When I moved to New York, I soon began storytelling – it was a wonderful combination of theater and teaching. As I began focusing on Jewish folk tales, I observed many people wanting to go deeper to explore the true messages of these stories. This reaction to the stories influenced me a great deal in my decision to pursue a doctorate in clinical psychology.

At about the same time, I was dealing with chronic pain that resulted from a car accident. After trying all traditional methods to alleviate the pain from the whiplash, I sought alternatives that I never would have considered in the past. I simply wasn't ready to accept my doctor's opinion that I would have to live with this pain for the rest of my life. I became interested in working with people who also were experiencing chronic pain. I thought, if I have these letters after my name, Ph.D., maybe people will come to me for treatment and be open to learning some of the alternative ways I had discovered through my journey.

In 2001, I happened to hear a woman talk about her positive experience with meditation. I then decided to try it by attending a meditation retreat and was delighted to discover how healing it was. I realized that I didn't need to visit a therapist or have a massage to feel better. Rather, as I closed my eyes, breathed, and focused on the moment, the world opened up and unfolded before me. Meditation is a window into just *being* in the present moment – without worrying about the past or the future. I love teaching skeptics, because I was one. I advise people to be open enough just to try it and see what happens. You may find you get to know yourself in a different way, perhaps even seeing yourself and the world around you with a little more compassion and lightheartedness.

*Vered Hankin was interviewed in the kitchen of her Lakeview home on August 10, 2010. Her birthday is November 6, 1973.*

## Favorites

**MOVIE**
*Whale Rider* (2002), a drama directed by Niki Caro. Based on the novel of the same name by Witi Ihimaera, this beautiful film brings to life folklore, hope, a powerful heroine, and a beautiful story in a magical setting.

**PLAY**
*Rent,* a rock musical with music and lyrics by Jonathan Larson. Every time I saw it, I kept thinking I wouldn't like it. But it continually swept me away. I find it energizing and healing.

**POET**
Shel Silverstein. Both silly and brilliant, he wrote *A Light in the Attic, Where the Sidewalk Ends, The Giving Tree,* and many other classics.

**QUOTATION**
"Life is no brief candle to me. It is a sort of splendid torch which I have got a hold of for the moment, and I want to make it burn as brightly as possible before handing it on to future generations."
— GEORGE BERNARD SHAW, IRISH PLAYWRIGHT

"*Life is no brief candle to me.*"

Brooke Hummer Mower Photography

# T. Gunny Harboe

## Preservation Architect

A pressing sense of stewardship mingles with a romantic nature to sustain his joy in restoring treasures of times gone by.

*Gunny Harboe heads an architecture firm specializing in historic preservation and sustainable design. This architect, with a special fondness for the treasures of the past, is the driving force behind the heralded restorations of several of Chicago's iconic structures, including the Rookery and Reliance buildings, Mies van der Rohe's S.R. Crown Hall at IIT, and Louis Sullivan's Carson Pirie Scott and Company Building. In 2006, he completed a restoration master plan for Frank Lloyd Wright's Unity Temple in Oak Park. Harboe holds an A.B. in History from Brown University. He earned his M.Arch. degree from Massachusetts Institute of Technology (MIT) and a M.Sc. in Historic Preservation from Columbia University.*

Because of both of my parents, I grew up with an appreciation for old things and their history – the stories that accompanied them. My father is a Danish immigrant whose ancestors were involved in the shipping business. When I was a child, paintings of these ships hung in our home as we moved from Evanston to Northfield to New Jersey and back again. My mother's family was English, Scotch-Irish, and French Huguenot. Her American roots trace back to a farm in Gap, Pennsylvania, where the eighteenth-century house still stands. She liked to share stories about her family through the many inherited possessions that filled our house, such as my great grandfather's Civil War rifle that hung in our kitchen. While it wasn't a conscious choice to do so, I thought a lot about how all of these things related to me and how they connected me to my ancestors.

At age eight, I flew to Denmark, alone, for the summer. My grandfather took me to Kronborg Castle, where *Hamlet* was set. It brought the country alive for me, and I imagined what it must have been like 300 years before. Although the castle was very old, I connected with it strongly. Later, after high school, on an extended stay to study Danish at a folk high school in Denmark, I developed a love of learning for learning's sake that remains with me today.

In college, I learned about the concept of *material culture*, a term used by archaeologists as a non-specific way to refer to the artifacts or other concrete things left by past cultures. I became fascinated with the idea that you could get a window on the past through a detailed examination of things that are left behind – like my family's possessions. I don't deny for a moment that my interest in all of this goes back to my own romantic notions; that's a strong driver for me.

As an intern architect of age thirty-three, I was responsible for the restoration aspects of renovating one of the most historically significant buildings in Chicago, the Rookery. [Note: Located at 209 S. LaSalle St., the building is a Chicago and National Historic Landmark. Designed by Burnham & Root, the Rookery was completed in 1888. Frank Lloyd Wright redesigned the two-story, skylit lobby in 1905.] While in architecture school, I'd tried to look in the windows during the time that the Rookery was closed up. Never in my wildest fantasy did I think that someday I would be able to restore that building.

Preserving our collective cultural heritage is important, particularly in Chicago, where it has international significance. We need to give it a life that extends beyond ourselves. The significance goes back to stewardship of these buildings that were created by humans, in the past, that tell us something about who we are today. That story needs to be told to those in the future.

I'm not a religious person, but I do believe that spirituality – however it is expressed – is essential to being human. One place that is spiritually significant to me is Frank Lloyd Wright's Unity Temple. Wright's powerful use of space and light created a place of worship that is incredibly moving. It also gives me a sense of connection to him and to that time in our history.

*Gunny Harboe was interviewed at the offices of Harboe Architects, located at 140 S. Dearborn St. in Chicago, on April 6, 2011. His birthday is October 3, 1955.*

---

## Favorites

### BOOK
*Sarum: The Novel of England* by Edward Rutherfurd. The book relates the country's story from the perspective of several English families in Salisbury, stretching from prehistoric times to the creation and development of England.

### MUSIC
"Kind of Blue" (1959), an influential album by jazz musician Miles Davis.

### PLACE
The Upper Valley of Vermont. The natural beauty, the history, and the architecture all combine to make it a special place.

### POET
Gary Snyder. He's a Pulitzer Prize-winning writer associated with Buddhist philosophies, the Beat movement, and the environment.

### QUOTATION
"These old buildings do not belong to us only, they belong to our forefathers and they will belong to our descendants unless we play them false. They are not in any sense our own property to do as we like with them. We are only trustees for those that come after us."
— WILLIAM MORRIS, ENGLISH TEXTILE DESIGNER, ARTIST, WRITER, AND LIBERTARIAN SOCIALIST

*"We are only trustees..."*

# Leslie Hindman

## Auction House CEO

From a lock of Elvis's hair to a $632,000, ten-carat diamond, every treasure's story slakes this entrepreneur's thirst for life itself.

*In 1982, twenty-seven-year-old Leslie Hindman founded her company, Leslie Hindman Auctioneers. Now the fifth-largest company of its kind in the U.S., the enterprise is experiencing substantial growth, thanks in large part to the global access the Internet provides to one-of-a-kind auction items. Her company has conducted many significant and highly publicized auctions, including memorabilia from the historic Comiskey Park, the Chicago Stadium, and the Schwinn Family Bicycle Collection. In 1991, Leslie Hindman Auctioneers received international recognition for the discovery of a previously unknown still life by Vincent van Gogh. Selling for $1.43 million, the painting catapulted the firm to the forefront of the world auction scene. Hindman also operates locations in Denver, Colorado; Detroit, Michigan; Milwaukee, Wisconsin; and in Naples and Palm Beach, Florida.*

My fondest childhood memories are associated with being a student at Avery Coonley School in Downers Grove from fifth through eighth grades. The classes were small and very special. For example, every day for a week during assembly, a different teacher would speak on her area of expertise, telling us about everything from the genius of Mozart to the splitting of the atom. Even today, looking back, much of what I know I learned at Avery Coonley. [Note: According to its website, the small, historic progressive school educates gifted children.] Many memorable teachers influenced me, particularly my French teacher, Madame Storm, who was elegant, beautiful, and warm. When Madame took a group of students to Paris when I was thirteen, that life-changing experience stimulated a love of travel and a desire to learn all I could about the world.

I went to France and Belgium every summer during my teen years. At thirteen, my parents took us to Ireland and Morocco. It was eye-opening for a girl from Hinsdale, Illinois, to watch a snake charmer perform in a Moroccan marketplace. My parents exposed us to a wide range of experiences, and they wanted all four of their kids to lead interesting lives. My father used to stand over our cribs when we were babies and say, "Talk, talk! We don't want any introverted kids," [laughs]. I am somewhat restless, though, and there's a part of me that envies people who are content to stay put in one place. I've moved sixteen times since the age of eighteen.

While I loved to travel, school was not my thing. I attended Pine Manor Junior College, the Sorbonne in Paris, and Indiana University – but I quit college just short of graduating. I moved home to Hinsdale and worked downtown at the offices of

Merrill Lynch. One day, the "big boss," Jack Scott, called me into his office and asked me why I was working there. When I replied that it was because I needed a job, he said he could see that I was a nice, intelligent young woman . . . with absolutely no interest in finance. He was kind enough to take the time to help me explore how I might get hired in a field I really liked, which was the art world. Jack Scott suggested I find a job, any job, in a gallery. I was incredibly fortunate to be hired as an assistant to Catharine Hamilton, who opened the first Sotheby's location outside of New York – here in Chicago in 1977.

I immediately fell in love with everything about the auction business. It's incredibly fascinating – the people, the fast pace, and learning how and why people collect the things they do. Auctions represent both the history of people and of objects. Many people don't realize it, but auctions offer a great way to learn about something you're interested in – from antique porcelain to vintage clothing. Anybody can attend at no cost, with rare exceptions, and you don't have to be wealthy or formally dressed to participate. These days, many of our bids are received online or by telephone.

The main reason I am successful is that I work harder than anyone I've ever met. In his bestselling book *Outliers,* Malcolm Gladwell's research validates that you must invest approximately 10,000 hours to become a true expert at something, whether it be hockey, playing piano, or anything else. His theory, which I believe to be true, is that if you work and work and work, you *will* achieve success. I started my auction house at age twenty-seven for two reasons: first, I couldn't think of anything else I wanted to do, and second, there wasn't one of any size and stature in the Midwest.

Many people believed in me, tutored me, and backed me financially. I truly believe I was born lucky and that good fortune has followed me throughout life.

*Leslie Hindman was interviewed on March 6, 2012, at her company headquarters, a warehouse overflowing with every imaginable treasure from Venetian urns to nineteenth-century oil paintings, on West Lake Street in Chicago. Her birthday is December 1, 1954.*

## Favorites

**BOOK**
*Working: People Talk About What They Do All Day and How They Feel About What They Do* by Studs Terkel.

**MOVIE**
*A Thousand Clowns* (1962), directed by Fred Coe and based on the play by Herb Gardner. I loved the fact that the main character, Murray, played by Jason Robards, wanted to avoid having a conventional job.

**PLACE**
Paris. I love everything about it. Who doesn't?

**SONG**
The Shaker hymn, "Simple Gifts," which is heard in Aaron Copland's "Appalachian Spring." When I hear it, I am reminded of how I should run my life.

**QUOTATION**
"No gain, no risk, no reward."
— AUTHOR UNKNOWN

" *No gain, no risk, no reward.* "

# Jamels James

## Founder, Leading India's Future Today (LIFT)

His loyal supporters at Old St. Pat's are committed to elevating talented, motivated, underprivileged children in southern India.

*Father Jamels James grew up in Pettai, a small village in southern India. He founded LIFT in 2004. Chancellor of the Palayamkottai Diocese in India, James is a parish priest serving seven churches in India. He lived in Chicago for twelve years and returns to the city regularly.*

*Operating out of Tamil Nadu in southern India, the nonprofit organization is committed to developing leadership excellence within the youth of the region – regardless of background, caste, or religious tradition. LIFT strives to raise the aspirations and leadership skills of less fortunate children to position them to transform their society by combating poverty and unemployment and improving the overall health of the region. LIFT is primarily funded by Chicagoans, particularly the parishioners of Old St. Pat's Church in the West Loop.*

By age twelve, I knew that I would become a priest; serious preparation began at seventeen. In 1994, when I came to Chicago to further my studies, I attended Loyola University and Northwestern University. At the same time, I was a chaplain and/or a priest at the Illinois Institute of Technology, St. James Church, Michael Reese Hospital, and Old St. Pat's Church, the last of which became particularly important in my life.

By the end of my time as an academic, I'd run into many dead ends and my soul wasn't being nourished. Although I didn't recognize it then, I was depressed and experiencing a midlife crisis. I sought spiritual counseling from a number of people. Father Bill Creed, a Jesuit priest and a professor at Loyola, helped me work through the darkness by challenging me to quit the academic life and take on something much larger than myself.

The best things in life just happen; you can't make them happen. That's the message of Parker Palmer's book *Let Your Life Speak: Listening for the Voice of Vocation.* His approach really changed my perspective. I realized that the question isn't, "What do I want to do with my life?" Rather, it is, "What does life want to do with *me*?"

After two years of struggling to find a larger purpose, one day I woke up with complete clarity and the idea for LIFT. It was like the Old Testament story of Jacob wrestling with God. Working with three other priests, LIFT evolved from the question: "What is the one thing that we could do in India that would make the biggest impact?"

There are so many problems – among them, malnutrition, child labor, the genocide of girls, and the dowry system. We decided to focus on developing the capabilities of youth so that each one can eventually make a contribution to society in his or her particular area of talent and expertise.

India is an ancient country with a very young population. Sixty percent of its people are younger than fourteen. But so much of the potential of the youth is being wasted. Many children don't go to school. Instead, they work in the fields or in factories that produce matches and fireworks. Through LIFT, we're creating the space, place, and opportunity for young people to excel.

Our Chicago supporters have taken me, and the children of LIFT, into their homes. One night, when a group of Chicagoans was visiting us in India, we all sang, danced, and laughed together after dinner. I remember thinking, if there is a heaven, then this is what it should be like . . . a place where people from different countries, colors, faiths, and ages can interact as one while joyously connecting at a deeper level where artificial boundaries all disappear.

*Father Jamels James was interviewed in the rectory at Old St. Pat's Church in Chicago on June 22, 2010. His birthday is November 27, 1962.*

## Favorites

**BOOKS**
*Will the Real Me Please Stand Up: 25 Guidelines for Good Communication* by John Powell and *The Wounded Healer: Ministry in Contemporary Society* by Henri Nouwen.

**MOVIE**
*Gandhi* (1982), directed by Richard Attenborough. I like how the film communicates that for Gandhi, there was no separation between the sacred and the secular. He made religion a springboard for political involvement.

**PASTIME**
I love people-watching at places where loved ones reunite – like airports and train stations. People are the faces of God, and God is present everywhere in humanity.

**PLACE**
Old St. Pat's is my home. Many generations have prayed here for more than 150 years, and their souls remain present.

**QUOTATION**
"A vocation is the place where our deep gladness meets the world's deep need."
— FREDERICK BUECHNER, AMERICAN WRITER AND THEOLOGIAN

*"the place where our deep gladness meets..."*

# Kathy Kelly

Peace Activist

Three-time nominee for the Nobel Peace Prize is "insanely optimistic" about the possibility of a war-free future.

*Kathy Kelly co-founded* Voices in the Wilderness *(1996-2005), an organization formed to "nonviolently challenge the economic warfare being waged against the people of Iraq."* Voices in the Wilderness *organized seventy delegations to travel to Iraq between 1996 and 2003. Kelly visited Iraq twenty-seven times to bring medicine to Iraqi families, meet with United Nations representatives, and act as a voice for people "who had no voice" and "whose children were dying in their arms." She now co-coordinates* Voices for Creative Nonviolence, *an organization started in 2005 "with deep, long-standing roots in active nonviolent resistance to U.S. war-making."*

*Kelly received a bachelor's from Loyola University and a master's in Religious Education from the Chicago Theological Seminary. A three-time nominee for the Nobel Peace Prize, she has been described as probably the most respected leader in the American peace movement. Kelly co-authored* Prisoners on Purpose: A Peacemakers' Guide to Jails and Prison *and co-edited* War and Peace in the Gulf. *She is also the author of* Other Lands Have Dreams: From Baghdad to Pekin Prison.

I always assumed I'd be a nun. Growing up in the Garfield Ridge neighborhood on the Southwest Side, nuns were the only "professional people" we knew. Doctors and lawyers didn't live in our neighborhood. I was enthralled by the nuns but changed my mind about my future when I was a junior at Loyola University. By that time, nuns were moving into apartments, adopting street wear, and, in some ways, living like everyone else. I shared an apartment with two sisters for several years and joined in their work in our impoverished neighborhood in Chicago's Uptown neighborhood. But I didn't enter religious life.

I am still drawn to the lives religious women lead. One quality that attracted me as a child and still impresses me is that nuns are not interested in accumulating personal wealth. My father was a Catholic high school teacher and my mother had been an indentured servant in Ireland. As one of six kids, acquiring wealth never occurred to me.

When I was getting my master's degree at the Chicago Theological Seminary, I realized I wanted to work with poor people. But I didn't encounter them living in Hyde Park, so a professor I admired suggested I go "up north" to a soup kitchen. I ended up at Saint Thomas Canterbury parish in Uptown, where I met a great group of committed people. It was a spiritual turning point for me: I learned that it would not be difficult to find a coherence between my core beliefs and values and the actions I could take to live them out.

One of my first important mentors, Karl Meyer, also was my husband for thirteen years. Karl was a protégé of Dorothy Day. In the 1930s, Day helped establish the Catholic Worker movement, a nonviolent, pacifist organization that continues to combine direct aid for the poor and homeless with nonviolent direct action on their behalf. I became a war tax resister, reducing my salary to beneath the taxable income level.

I've been frightened many times in my life. One of the scariest times, initially, was when I went to federal prison in Lexington, Kentucky, for nine months in 1989. I'd planted corn on top of nuclear missile sites on five separate occasions. One thing I know – that there's a war against the poor in this country – is particularly obvious in prison. Through the prison experience, I was emboldened, and it bolstered my belief that I could survive something very difficult. The most onerous aspect of a term in federal prison is the length of sentencing. Interestingly, the women I met in prison were not frightening.

I am insanely optimistic about the future. I would not rule out the possibility that in one hundred years, people will look back at our time and wonder, "What were they *thinking*?" By that time, history – as well as social/cultural movements – may be at a stage resembling the abolitionary movement that helped end slavery. There may be a tipping point when people declare, "We don't want to live like that anymore." Interestingly, there's now even talk about World War II and whether there might have been other solutions to the problems of the time.

The book that best describes a life of committed activism is *From Yale to Jail: The Life Story of a Moral Dissenter* by David Dellinger. Its message is that acting in response to the major ethical questions of our time requires risk. Recompense comes in the form of relationships and the opportunity to live in accordance with your beliefs.

*Kathy Kelly was interviewed in the kitchen of her home in the Uptown neighborhood on April 19, 2010. Her birthday is December 10, 1952.*

## Favorites

**BOOK**

*The Remains of the Day* by Kazuo Ishiguro. It is "a dream of a book: a beguiling comedy of manners that evolves almost magically into a profound and heartrending study of personality, class, and culture," according to a *New York Times* book review.

**MUSIC/SOUND**

The songs of Leonard Cohen, Gregorian chants, and the Muslim Call to Prayer.

**PLACES**

The streets of Al Jumhuriyah in Al Basra in southern Iraq. I hope to walk there again someday. In Chicago, my favorite park is the one behind the Museum of Science and Industry.

**QUOTATION**

"We are all part of one another."
– BARBARA DEMING, AMERICAN FEMINIST AND ADVOCATE OF NONVIOLENT SOCIAL CHANGE

"*We are all part of one another.*"

Photo by Cetta Kenney

# Jim Kenney

## Co-Founder and Executive Director, Common Ground

Committed to enhancing peace and harmony, he advances a better understanding of our neighbors – all around the globe.

*It's challenging to try to label Jim Kenney, and one gets the impression he likes it that way. A longtime teacher and activist, in 1975 he co-founded Common Ground with his mentor, Ron Miller (who died in 2010). Deerfield-based Common Ground is a center for inquiry, study, and dialogue whose primary concern is the human quest for understanding and the pursuit of human significance. With 7,000 people on its mailing list, Common Ground speaks to individuals of every stripe in its focus on the world's great cultural, philosophical, religious, and spiritual traditions.*

*While Common Ground represents the bedrock of Kenney's foundation, he long ago expanded into more global endeavors. For two decades, he's been a recognized leader in the global movement for interreligious and intercultural understanding. Through his intense involvement with several organizations – including the Parliament of the World's Religions and the Interreligious Engagement Project – he has helped launch a worldwide interreligious movement. These days, Kenney is focusing on the concepts of interconnectedness and the enhancement of global understanding. His latest book is* Thriving in the Crosscurrent: Clarity and Hope in a Time of Cultural Sea Change.

I was the oldest of seven kids. People who knew me well often encouraged me to become a priest because I was an active altar boy, but I knew that wasn't for me. While attending Regis Jesuit High School in Aurora, Colorado, my Greek teacher was Ron Miller. We stayed in touch, later attended graduate school together in the field of comparative religion at Northwestern University, and then began Common Ground.

We saw the need for Common Ground because people had very little opportunity to learn about the religions of the world, and they *were* curious about experiences beyond their own kind. I held out for expanding beyond religion, spirituality, and philosophy to include culture and multiculturalism. In total, we've offered more than 500 distinct classes over the years, including *Henry David Thoreau – America's Conscience, Looking Back on "The White City" – the 1893 World Columbian Exposition in Chicago,* and *The Tea Party and American Conservatism.*

Degreed professionals teach almost all of our classes. We're very open to new ideas at Common Ground, and before introducing an idea, it is carefully vetted by others, as well as myself, to ensure its soundness. I've been asked why we don't give "equal time" to groups such as Fundamentalists, but I believe they have their own pulpits.

People are astonished to learn that Chicago is the most religiously diverse city on the planet, according to Diana Eck, a professor of comparative religion and director of the Pluralism Project at Harvard University. London or Los Angeles seems the obvious choice, but Chicago takes that title based on the number of members of diverse religious communities that live here.

I advocate vocally for interreligious pluralism, the idea that more than one tradition can be completely valid. I believe that people of faith, whatever that faith may be, ought to at least entertain the idea that the faith tradition of someone across the world is equally authentic. One particular belief system is not right or wrong. When I think about people of my era, we had so much to get over – beginning with racism, homophobia, and sexism. Most of today's young people, on the other hand, don't think much about the color or religion or class of the people they know; rather, these individuals are simply *their friends*.

This level of acceptance stems from a heightened degree of globalism. I ask people in my classes to look at their own view of the world versus that of their grandparents. It would have been impossible for our grandparents to think in the global way that many of us do today. Fifty years ago, the only global issues were war and international trade; today, that list includes the environment, poverty, health issues, and much more. This kind of thinking is evidence of *cultural evolution*, and it's the organizing principle of my life.

When one starts thinking about all of the challenges inherent in interconnected problems and areas of concern, it naturally leads to the principle of universal human rights. First, there are certain things we must do for *all* human beings and second, there are other things that must never be done to *any* human beings. These values date back to Eleanor Roosevelt's 1948 "Universal Declaration of Human Rights."

We're in a sea change era now – a time when change is dramatically heightened. There is an enormous opportunity for positive change, but it's daunting, too. The way people feel about how the world is going depends on how they react when they wake up in the morning. Are they riding the "old wave" and afraid to let go of it? Or are they ready to start riding the "new wave"? The latter option is very exciting.

*Jim Kenney was interviewed at the offices of Common Ground in north suburban Deerfield on May 11, 2012. His birthday is July 9, 1947.*

## Favorites

**BOOKS**

*The Lord of the Rings,* the epic fantasy trilogy by English philologist J. R. R. Tolkien. I've read it nearly thirty times because I'm fascinated by the story's incredible complexity and the moral issues it raises.

**MUSIC**

My favorite band is the Dillards, and my favorite of their songs is "Sundown."

**PERFORMERS**

Meryl Streep and Anthony Hopkins. Whenever I watch them, I always forget they're acting.

**QUOTATION**

"Every religion is superior to every other by virtue of something it does best."
— FRITHJOF SCHUON, SWISS PHILOSOPHER

66 *Every religion is superior to every other...* 99

# Tim King

## Founder, Urban Prep Academies

A trailblazer garners national attention with his exceptional approach to the education of young African American men.

*Self-described as a "hardheaded optimist," Tim King grew up in the exclusive far South Side Chicago neighborhood known as "Pill Hill." He was embraced by a large, close-knit extended family that was highly educated and economically successful. As a teen, King was a standout at Saint Ignatius College Prep, a highly competitive Jesuit school located on Roosevelt Road. Later, after graduating from Georgetown University and Georgetown Law School, also Jesuit institutions, he defined his career in the classroom rather than the courtroom.*

*In 1994, King began a five-year tenure at Hales Franciscan High School, an all-male, Catholic, predominantly African American school on the South Side. He quickly assumed the school's presidency. Under his leadership, 100 percent of graduates were admitted to college. A few years later, King founded the nonprofit entity that soon launched Urban Prep Academies, a charter school operating under the aegis of the Chicago Public Schools. It's a network of three all-male public high schools with campuses in Englewood, Bronzeville, and on the Near West Side. When King was a guest on Oprah Winfrey's TV show, she described him as "an angel" and donated $750,000 to Urban Prep.*

*In June 2013, the 150 members of the graduating class tossed their mortarboards joyfully skyward as they grabbed the bar set by the three previous graduating classes: 100 percent of them had been accepted to college.*

My great grandparents came to Chicago when they were very young. From early on, our family focused on education as the key to professional, social, and economic advancement. My mother is a retired educator, and my father owned a company, UBM, that was, at the time, the largest African American–owned construction firm in Illinois. He sometimes joked that UBM stood for "U Better Move." I'm the third generation of my family to attend college.

Saint Ignatius provided me with a fantastic educational experience. I believe it was – and still is – the best Catholic high school in the city, if not the country. Of course [laughs] I'm not at all biased. The Jesuits emphasize a particular way of thinking that incorporates a high level of introspection, self-reflection, and the articulation of ideas. Even when students present ideas that are contrary to the fairly restrictive thinking of the Catholic Church, they are encouraged to express their thoughts and build cases for them.

The dream of creating Urban Prep Academies evolved from my years as president of Hales Franciscan. I believed that there ought to be a *tuition-free* college prep high school focusing on African American boys – especially those who were economically disadvantaged.

Getting Urban Prep off the ground is the biggest obstacle I've overcome. My proposal to start the school was rejected twice before it was accepted, and I almost gave up. However, in my mind, I'd already determined the motto, "We Believe," as a core element of the school's philosophy. So when I was ready to quit, a friend of mine challenged me by asking, "Isn't your motto supposed to be, 'We Believe'?" I listened to her, and at last, our third application to Chicago Public Schools was accepted. The creation of Urban Prep reinforced what my parents and the Jesuits had always emphasized: a responsibility to effect positive change, particularly because I'd been given a fortunate life. The Jesuit creed is: "Men and women for others."

The biggest challenge we face at Urban Prep is the lack of preparation evident in so many of our students when they come to us. As they prepare to start high school, some read at only a fourth-grade level. We have to determine how to accelerate them at least one and one-half grade levels every year in order for them to begin to equal their peers at other schools. When they graduate, some are *still behind,* but their work ethic is so strong they go forward with the firm belief that, "If I work hard enough, I *will* catch up."

Our school culture emphasizes the "four R's" – respect, responsibility, relationship, and ritual. The concept of respect plays a particularly critical role among African American males. Yet many of these young men have never experienced what it's like to be treated respectfully. All of our students are addressed as "Mr. (surname)" or "sir." This may seem minor, but it affects them in an incredibly positive way.

[Note: Urban Prep grads routinely express extraordinary emotion about their experiences with Tim King and the Urban Prep team. Their gratitude is evident in statements like, "Urban Prep has been my mother and my father," and "Mr. King never gave up on his ideas, so we don't give up on ours." Says Tim King, "We all have different gifts. I may not be able to play the piano or be a calculus whiz, but I do know how to inspire and persuade; that's my gift."]

*Tim King was interviewed at the administrative offices of Urban Prep Academies in the Loop on July 2, 2012. His birthday is June 15, 1967.*

---

## Favorites

**BOOKS**
The Harry Potter series by J. K. Rowling. I love these books because they're about a boy who is special but doesn't know that he's special. When he finds that out, he doesn't rest on his laurels.

**MOVIE**
*It's a Wonderful Life* (1946), directed by Frank Capra. It illustrates my belief that we are all so connected.

**PLACE**
My parents' house. It's where I grew up and where they've lived for forty years.

**POEM**
"A Dream Deferred" by Langston Hughes. Here are the opening lines:

"What happens to a dream deferred?
 Does it dry up
 like a raisin in the sun?"

**QUOTATION**
"Try not. Do or do not. There is no try."
— YODA IN *STAR WARS: EPISODE 5 – THE EMPIRE STRIKES BACK.*

*"Try not. Do or do not. There is no try."*

Photo by Kathy Richland

# Alex Kotlowitz

## Journalist and Nonfiction Storyteller

His "journalism of empathy" offers keen insights into poverty, racism, and other societal issues.

*Alex Kotlowitz, journalist and author, is best known for the influential nonfiction bestseller* There Are No Children Here. *Published in 1991, it is the recipient of numerous awards and was named one of the 150 most important books of the twentieth century by the New York Public Library. Kotlowitz's 2004 volume,* Never a City So Real, *is a collection of contemporary stories from Chicago, his adopted hometown. The* Chicago Sun-Times *described it as "a fine successor to Nelson Algren's* Chicago: City on the Make *as a song to our rough-and-tumble, broken-nosed city."*

*His documentary "The Interrupters," a collaboration with producer/director Steve James, premiered at the Sundance Film Festival in 2011 and later aired on PBS's "FRONTLINE." A writer-in-residence at Northwestern University, Kotlowitz graduated from Wesleyan University in Middletown, Connecticut. He is the recipient of eight honorary degrees and the John LaFarge Memorial Award for Interracial Justice given by New York's Catholic Interracial Council.*

I grew up in the '60s in what was then a richly diverse area of New York City. The Upper West Side was mixed by class and by race. My mom, who was deeply involved in the civil rights and anti-war movements, provided me with my political sensibility. She took me to my first anti-war rally when I was thirteen. My father, a writer, gave me what has become one of the staples of my life – my love of reading. Our house was filled with books, floor to ceiling.

I stumbled into becoming a writer after realizing that biology, which I loved for its sense of discovery, not unlike journalism, wasn't for me. In college, I took a semester off and, by chance, wound up working at a settlement house in Atlanta. It was my first exposure to the deep and profound poverty in our cities. The experience was simultaneously unsettling and exhilarating as I encountered so many people who managed to remain erect and maintain their dignity. The time there was transformative.

Later, I became involved in the politics of Middletown, Connecticut, where I attended Wesleyan University. I was fortunate to have two mentors – older men who taught me a great deal about activism, city politics, and race. One was the union president at the local Pratt & Whitney plant and the other an activist at a public housing complex.

At twenty-one, I began writing for an alternative newspaper in Lansing, Michigan. I felt alive when I was telling stories. And my work pushed me into places I otherwise would never have reason to spend time. In 1984, *The Wall Street Journal* hired me, in Chicago, and I eventually carved out a niche for the paper writing about social issues. That's where I first wrote about Lafayette and Pharoah, the boys who lived at the Henry Horner housing projects and who were at the center of *There Are No Children Here*. [Note: The brothers were nine and twelve at the start of the two years Kotlowitz spent with them.] I'd never been to Chicago's housing projects before, but they were just a stone's throw from my then-office downtown. I was knocked off balance by the violence and the deplorable living conditions. It made me angry, even ashamed. How could I not know?

I wanted to tell the story of this community, and I figured that if I could really get into the heads of the boys and look at the world through their eyes, people would sit up and take notice. As a storyteller, I hope to take people to places they wouldn't necessarily venture. Lafayette and Pharoah are in their thirties now, and we're still quite close. The success of *There Are No Children Here* allowed me to pursue the stories that appeal to me. Some people ask why I write such "dark" stories, but I don't think of them that way. Instead, I marvel at the ability of people to emerge reasonably intact, sometimes with their heads held high, after fighting through such difficult circumstances.

Writing *Never a City So Real* made me fall back in love with Chicago. It's a collection of stories about people who are all outsiders, whether by politics, race, status, or sometimes just fate. I love this city with all its beauty, rawness, and contradictions. Richard Wright, who wrote *Native Son*, said about Chicago: "There is an open and raw beauty about it that seems either to kill or endow one with the spirit of life." I've seen it do both.

*Alex Kotlowitz was interviewed at the kitchen table of his home in Oak Park on May 16, 2011. His birthday is March 31, 1955.*

## Favorites

**BOOKS**

Among my top choices: Fyodor Dostoyevsky's novels, which helped me through my adolescence; *The Dollmaker* by Harriet Arnow, a 1954 novel about a family's migration from Appalachia to wartime Detroit; and *Common Ground: A Turbulent Decade in the Lives of Three American Families* by J. Anthony Lukas, which made me think, "Hey, this is what I'd like to do, write nonfiction as if it reads like a novel."

**NONPROFIT**

The Young Center for Immigrant Children's Rights. This is my wife's organization, which works to promote the best interests of immigrant children who have come to this country by themselves and then are detained by the immigration authorities.

**PLACE**

On water, canoeing. I find solace and rejuvenation there.

**QUOTATION**

I love the lyrics to the Bob Dylan song "Forever Young." Here are the closing lines:

"And may your song always be sung.
 May you stay forever young."

"*And may your song always be sung.*"

# Bill Kurtis

## Broadcaster/Documentarian and Entrepreneur

Kansan Renaissance Man advises us to develop the talents we've been given . . . whatever they may be.

*Bill Kurtis's life is characterized by a distinguished career including a thirty-year tenure with CBS Television. He covered many celebrated trials of the '60s and '70s; among them, that of convicted mass murderer Charles Manson. Kansas-educated, Kurtis earned his B.S. in Journalism at the University of Kansas and a J.D. from Washburn University School of Law. He and his partner, Donna La Pietra, divide their time between a downtown home and one in Lake County's Mettawa, a village that is dedicated to preserving open lands and low-density residential development.*

*Kurtis spends as much time as possible on his Red Buffalo Ranch, located in Sedan, Kansas. His business interests include the documentary production company Kurtis Productions; Tall Grass Beef Company, a purveyor of meat from cattle that is 100 percent grass-fed, antibiotic- and hormone-free, and raised on the Kurtis Ranch; and ownership interest in broadcast stations. He is the recipient of numerous humanitarian, journalism, and broadcasting awards.*

My dad was an aviation instructor in the U.S. Marine Corps. When he headed to the Pacific theater during WWII, I was fourteen. My mom and I went to live in Independence, Kansas, with my grandparents and I'd already moved nine times. While it was difficult to be continually uprooted, there were benefits. I learned to make new friends, adapt easily, and read situations quickly.

Kansas is the home of my heart. It's a magical place because of the tallgrass prairie, and it's similar to Africa in that way. You stand on the land, look around, and feel you belong there. I feel better when I'm in Kansas, and the ranch is something I want to protect and preserve. My ranch, Red Buffalo Ranch, takes its name from the Osage Indian term "fire on the prairie." It's there that I've developed my own philosophy, whether you call that animism or something else. [Note: Animism is the philosophical, religious, or spiritual idea that souls or spirits exist not only in humans but also in animals, plants, rocks, and natural phenomena, such as thunder, and in geographic features such as mountains, rivers, or other entities of the natural environment.]

I've had encounters with many religions, and one lesson that arises repeatedly is that we all have both good and bad within us. When I was covering the hostage crisis in Tehran in 1980, an angry mob was chasing my crew and me down the street yelling anti-American sentiments. Frightened, we entered the shop of a pharmacist. The gang was banging on the door to get in. The pharmacist said, "I am a Muslim, and I don't necessarily like Americans. But my religion dictates that when you are in my home or place of business, I must give you protection and safe passage." He went outside, parted the crowd, and put us in a taxi. We sped away. The one word that comes to mind with Islam is "devout," and my thoughts on the Muslim religion changed after that encounter.

Once we were in the Amazon following an ethnobotanist while making a documentary segment for "The New Explorers" program. He was looking for plants to use as the basis for new medications. Towards the end of our stay, I saw people lined up to receive a little white pill. When I asked what it was, I learned it was aspirin. Think of it: With that one little white pill, we destroyed a culture's entire basis for treating and healing itself. And what did we miss out on as a result?

I hate injustice. I wrote *The Death Penalty on Trial: Crisis in American Justice* to uncover a broken system. There are many reasons why – biased judges, many prosecutors who aren't seeking justice but simply want to win, and defense attorneys who are ill-prepared. That's not the way it's supposed to be. The introduction of DNA into the process uncorked the bad genie; there was a realization that many innocent people had been wrongfully convicted. Fortunately, there are many people within the system that are working to correct some of these problems.

What really moves me is individual talent. This is almost the meaning of life: Experience everything, but perfect those talents you've been given. I have a deep voice, but that wouldn't have done me any good if I'd been a lumberjack. Perhaps someone else has a talent for helping others. Whatever it is, do it.

*Bill Kurtis was interviewed at his office in the River North neighborhood on August 24, 2010. His birthday is September 21, 1940.*

---

## Favorites

**MOVIE**

*The Searchers* (1956), directed by John Ford. Set during the Texas-Indian Wars, the film is based on a 1954 novel by Alan Le May. John Wayne stars as a middle-aged Civil War veteran who spends years looking for his abducted niece.

**NONPROFITS**

Everything from the Nature Conservancy to the Rehabilitation Institute of Chicago.

**PLACE**

A tree house at our home in far north suburban Mettawa. Ten feet by ten feet in size, it's like an observation deck over a watering hole you'd find in Africa.

**POET**

Rudyard Kipling. He's inspirational, especially "If." Here are the closing lines:

"If you can fill the unforgiving minute
  With sixty seconds' worth of distance run
  Yours is the Earth and everything that's in it
  And – which is more – you'll be a Man, my son."

**QUOTATION**

"People say that what we're all seeking is a meaning for life. I think that what we're really seeking is an experience of being alive, so that our life experiences on the purely physical plane will have resonance within our innermost being and reality, so that we can actually feel the rapture of being alive."
— JOSEPH CAMPBELL, AMERICAN MYTHOLOGIST, WRITER, AND LECTURER

"*...feel the rapture of being alive.*"

# Martha Lavey

## Artistic Director, Steppenwolf Theatre Company

Manifesting her creativity through the company's philosophy that actors are like family members – each one irreplaceable and with inalienable rights.

*Martha Lavey has been the artistic director of Steppenwolf Theatre Company since 1995. While leading this highly acclaimed troupe, she also has appeared in several of its productions, including* Middletown, Endgame, *and* Aunt Dan and Lemon. *During Lavey's tenure as artistic director, Steppenwolf productions have transferred to Broadway, the National Theatre in London, Sydney Theatre Company, theaters in Galway and Dublin, and to theaters throughout the U.S. She has received the Sarah Siddons Award, Alumni Merit Award, and an honorary doctorate from Northwestern University, where she earned her doctorate in performance studies.*

Growing up in a family of seven children shaped me by conveying mindfulness about one's place in the world. And specifically, my parents' emphasis on service and education created an expectation about how one conducts herself. There was never any pressure to prove myself financially. Rather, I recall almost a perverse shunning of money. Consequently, when I decided to pursue a life in theater, there wasn't even a whisper about how I would survive financially, which was very freeing.

Two of the games I played from a young age involved either staging plays or setting up a schoolroom in the basement of our home. There was always a notion that I would either act or teach. By some incredible stroke of good fortune, I have a leadership role in a remarkable theatrical institution, and I have taught acting and literature.

The small Catholic high school I attended offered few electives, but at my mom's suggestion, I signed up for drama. My teacher, Anne Knoll, offered me the role of Annie Sullivan in *The Miracle Worker*. She subsequently invited me on a trip to visit Northwestern University to further cultivate my theatrical interests. I later received both my B.A. in theater and a Ph.D. in performance studies from Northwestern. I still maintain a correspondence with Anne Knoll, who has been a major force in my life.

After completing undergraduate work, I enrolled in a scene study class at Steppenwolf. John Malkovich, my teacher, cast me in my first play at Steppenwolf Theatre Company. I loved Steppenwolf from the start. It's a unique place that builds itself around the artist, primarily the forty-three actors who comprise the ensemble. We experience repeated and repeatable relationships, and an actor is reassured in knowing he or she will return to perform with the same actors again.

The Steppenwolf culture reinforces that this is your home. You belong here, you are a family member, and you have rights. Actors feel far more empowered here than in many other theatrical environments. It's always been that way, owing to the uncanny wisdom and conviction of our founders – Terry Kinney, Jeff Perry, and Gary Sinise.

Fifteen years after arriving at Steppenwolf, I was offered the role of artistic director to continue the mission of the theater. Our vision is achieved through our core values of ensemble, innovation, and citizenship. We believe that the voice of the artist is a vital force in the discourse of our culture.

It is through the language of metaphor and in the arena of play that our soul is given utterance and our lives with others find common ground. We commit, through that expressiveness, to innovation. We dedicate ourselves to wakefulness, to the challenge and joy of liveliness. Finally, we commit, through these values, to citizenship: We own our role in the life of our shared communities – our audiences, our fellow artists, and our colleague American theaters.

Through many readings and experiences, I've come to understand the critical value of looking at a situation to discover what questions it wants you to ask. Learning about the significance of this realization has been a huge part of my intellectual and spiritual journey, one that also includes Buddhist thought and teachings. I was raised Catholic and although I do not attend church, the first thing I do every day is get down on my knees and express gratitude. I also take a prayer walk along Lake Michigan or practice a sitting meditation, which I've done for the past fifteen years.

Meditation helps immensely in my work. After I started practicing, I remember thinking, "Nothing has changed but everything is different." Sitting teaches so much, including to stop being so judgmental and reactive. Become more accepting of others and quit projecting stuff onto them. That's not to say I don't fail again and again, but I keep trying.

*Martha Lavey was interviewed on December 14, 2011, at the Steppenwolf Theatre Company's administrative office on North Avenue in Old Town. Her birthday is February 20, 1957.*

## Favorites

**BOOK**

*Always We Begin Again: The Benedictine Way of Living* by John McQuiston II. I return to this title again and again as a simple guideline for daily spiritual life.

**PLAYS**

*The Winter's Tale* production by Steppenwolf Theatre's Frank Galati – I love the philosophy it communicates; *Aunt Dan and Lemon*, a play by Wallace Shawn that bristles with intelligence; and ensemble member Tracy Letts's *August: Osage County*,★ for all that it has meant to this company.

**POET**

Mary Oliver. In the simplest ways, she finds the entire world holy.

**QUOTATION**

"We shall not cease from exploration, and the end of all our exploring will be to arrive where we started and know the place for the first time."
– AMERICAN POET T. S. ELIOT, "THE WASTE LAND"

★ *August: Osage County* was awarded the prestigious 2008 Pulitzer Prize for Drama.

“*We shall not cease from exploration...*”

# Hal Lewis

President and CEO, Spertus Institute for Jewish Learning and Leadership

Most people can learn to lead more effectively, he asserts.

*Hal M. Lewis, Ph.D., is the eighth president and CEO of Spertus, a ninety-year-old institution providing dynamic learning opportunities, rooted in Jewish wisdom and culture, that enable personal growth and the development of future community leaders. Like the soaring, expansive, and inviting structure that houses it at 610 S. Michigan Ave., Spertus is innovative in its public programming, exhibits, research facilities, degree programs, and more. Lewis also holds a faculty position as Professor of Contemporary Jewish Studies at Spertus, where he earned his Doctor of Jewish Studies Degree. Previously, he held a range of academic, administrative, and leadership roles at a variety of Jewish organizations in Ohio and New York, among other locales. Lewis's books are* From Sanctuary to Boardroom: A Jewish Approach to Leadership *and* Models and Meanings in the History of Jewish Leadership.

My parents were first-generation Americans. Their parents came from Europe, and my parents ran away from the religion of their parents. Living in Brooklyn and then moving to Long Island, New York, my mother and father assimilated, bought a house in the suburbs, and sent my brother, my sister, and me to public schools rather than to Jewish day schools.

We joined a synagogue for the same reason that families of all religions joined a formal place of worship – it was how you became Americanized. My parents were decidedly not observant, but we kids attended religious services every Saturday. For some reason, that fact continues to mystify every member of my family; something about that experience was positive for all of us kids. I don't think they really thought about it, but my parents made wise and strategic decisions in terms of what the contemporary Jewish community now understands as critical to the formation of Jewish identity.

There isn't a time when I *wasn't* involved in leadership – on learning, growing, reflecting on leadership experiences, and working with others. Despite what some people still believe, leadership *isn't about the leader alone.* Rather, it's about reciprocity and the relationship between – for example – manager *and* employee, student *and* teacher, or parent *and* child. It begins and ends with humility. Peter Drucker, who is considered the dean of leadership studies in America, famously said: "Approach problems with your ignorance." He meant that when we are humble enough to admit we don't know everything, we can ask the right questions in order to solve complicated problems.

There's a leadership theory that contends many leaders experience "crucible," or transformative, moments. I don't completely adhere to that way of thinking. Instead, I believe we are the product of our cumulative experiences. However, the closest I came to a crucible moment was when a volunteer leader with whom I worked closely said to me, "You are so good at your work. Why do you stay in the nonprofit sector?" For me, she threw down the gauntlet.

As a result, one of the driving forces of my career – including my academic work, my research, and how I hire – is to dispel the notion that those who work in the nonprofit sector do so because they couldn't make it in the so-called real world. Unfortunately, that notion still exists; just look at the disparities in salaries, benefits, and prestige between the corporate and the nonprofit arenas. But nothing could be further from the truth. Nonprofit professionals are talented, skilled, effective leaders who get things done.

The Hebrew word for leader is *manhig,* whose root means "behavior." Leadership is not about title, or physical attributes; it's about behavior. What this means is that leadership can come from anywhere in an organization; it is not limited to a certain type of person. The best example of this is Moses, Judaism's greatest leader. By all accounts, he should not have succeeded. He had a speech impediment and was a terrible orator. He was reticent and didn't want the job that God gave him in Exodus 4:10. Yet he went on to be the exemplary Jewish leader, whose *behavior* was marked by humility, compassion, boldness, a sense of service to others, tenacity, and selflessness.

For many of us, the biggest challenge we face is parenthood. The stakes are the highest, and the consequences are the most long-term. In order to grow leadership in others, good parents, like good leaders, must learn to *contract* a bit – *tzimtzum* in Hebrew, a term from Jewish mysticism. When God created the world, God chose to contract a bit of the divine self to allow room for human beings. As mothers and fathers, and leaders, we must follow that example.

*Hal Lewis was interviewed on July 9, 2012 in the boardroom of the Spertus Institute for Jewish Learning and Leadership, which offers magnificent views of Michigan Avenue and the city beyond. His birthday is January 13, 1953.*

# Favorites

**AUTHOR**
Pat Conroy. His novels, including *The Prince of Tides* and *The Great Santini*, are examples of brilliant storytelling.

**MOVIE**
*Eyes Wide Shut* (1999), directed by Stanley Kubrick. Film critic Roger Ebert described it as an erotic daydream about chances missed and opportunities avoided.

**PERFORMER**
Singer-songwriter Leonard Cohen. He is as dark as it gets, but his work is a metaphor for everything I treasure. Underlying all of the cynicism is a profound sense of optimism and hope.

**QUOTATION**
"For sudden the worst turns the best to the brave."
— ROBERT BROWNING, ENGLISH POET AND PLAYWRIGHT, FROM THE POEM "PROSPICE"

*"...the worst turns the best to the brave."*

# Ramsey Lewis

## Jazz Legend

After more than seven decades, he still revels in adding new twists to his repertoire.

*Composer and pianist Ramsey Lewis has been a musician for seventy-two of his seventy-six years (at this writing, in 2011). He represents the great diversity of music for which Chicago is so renowned. Lewis began captivating fans with his first album,* Ramsey Lewis and the Gentlemen of Swing, *by the Ramsey Lewis Trio. His chart toppers include "The In Crowd," "Hang On Sloopy," and "Wade in the Water."*

*A lifelong Chicagoan, Lewis has garnered three Grammy Awards and seven gold records. He was awarded the prestigious Lincoln Academy of Illinois "Laureate" in 1997 and was the recipient of the National Endowment for the Arts Jazz Masters Award in January, 2007. In addition to recording albums and performing live, Lewis is the artistic director of the Ravinia Festival's jazz series. He tours regularly with his quintet, featuring Henry Johnson on guitar, Joshua Ramos on bass, Charles Heath on drums, and Tim Gant on keyboards.*

I started taking lessons at age four. My father was the choir director at our church and, at his request, I began playing for the gospel choir at age nine. From the ages of four to fifteen, I was immersed in both gospel music and European classical music. Gospel music still is very important to me. I have about 800 songs on my iPod under the title "Sunday Morning Music," but I play them on other days of the week, too. A couple of titles that stick with me are Thomas A. Dorsey's "Precious Lord, Take My Hand" and "Pass Me Not, O Gentle Savior."

As a creative person, you are always changing. Your basic fingerprint is always there, but your interpretation of life's experiences affects how you live life – and how you create. People, events, and activities in your life resonate deeply, whether they are positive or negative. They affect your artistic expression and your being. Life is full of both blessings and lessons, and it's important to see the value in all of your experiences.

I started writing long-form music about five years ago, and it requires a different kind of creative process than writing melodic songs, many of which are just a few minutes in length. A few years ago, Ravinia Festival Chief Executive Officer Welz Kauffman suggested I compose a special piece in honor of Abraham

Lincoln's 200th birthday. It was daunting at first, but I did it by immersing myself in Lincoln. I visited the Lincoln Museum in Springfield and the Chicago History Museum to learn as much as I could about the man.

When I finally sat down to compose "Proclamation of Hope," it was like writing to pictures in my mind. Once I did the work, it wasn't so difficult. But that's how life is, isn't it? You believe the hill is higher than it actually is.

After performing the piece at Ravinia in June 2009, I was invited to do so at the Kennedy Center in Washington, D.C. Public television also broadcast the concert. It was all quite momentous. [Note: In writing about "Proclamation of Hope" the *Chicago Tribune* said, "What Lewis originally intended as a celebration of black music in America and Lincoln's role in igniting it eventually blossomed into an exploration of the links between Presidents Lincoln and Obama."]

Another long-form work yielded a meaningful moment that turned on a light for me. It happened in connection with a collaboration between the Joffrey Ballet and myself. When one of my sons came backstage after a performance, he said he'd realized that it was the first time I'd ever received a standing ovation without playing any of my hits. At most of my concerts, that's what the crowd wants to hear.

I was inspired by my wife of twenty years, Jan, in composing music to be performed by the Joffrey. In terms of long-form pieces, I'm not sure how far I could have gone down that road if it hadn't been for her. She is not only my muse; she is my sounding board. I titled that piece of music "To Know Her Is to Love Her."

*Ramsey Lewis was interviewed by telephone on May 9, 2011. His birthday is May 27, 1935.*

## Favorites

**BOOKS**

*A Course in Miracles* by Dr. Helen Schucman, which describes a philosophy of forgiveness including practical lessons and applications for the practice of forgiveness in daily life; *The Miracle of Mindfulness* by the Vietnamese Buddhist monk Thich Nhat Hahn, which is a classic volume written in 1974 that can help anyone to develop the mindfulness skills necessary to slow down and start living life in the present moment; and *Three Cups of Tea: One Man's Mission to Promote Peace . . . One School at a Time* by David Oliver Relin and Greg Mortenson.

**PERFORMERS**

Opera singer Renée Fleming; pianist and composer Vladimir Horowitz; jazz saxophonist and composer Charlie Parker; and jazz pianist Art Tatum.

**PLACE**

The place within oneself; that's where the kingdom of heaven lies.

**QUOTATION**

"Wherever you go, there you are."
— JON KABAT-ZINN, MEDITATION MASTER, FROM THE TITLE OF HIS CLASSIC BOOK

"*Wherever you go, there you are.*"

# James Lovell

## Apollo 13 Astronaut

The embodiment of "the right stuff," he is celebrated for saving the Apollo 13 mission from seemingly certain catastrophe.

*Esteemed as an American hero by a generation of Americans, Capt. James ("Jim") Lovell courageously captained the ill-fated NASA space mission that shook the world in 1970 and was later dramatized in the film "Apollo 13," based on Lovell's book* Lost Moon: The Perilous Voyage of Apollo 13. *The Moon-bound mission was aborted after an oxygen tank exploded, causing extreme damage to the spacecraft's fuel and oxygen supply. While the three-man crew never made it to the Moon, they pulled off a miraculous journey by returning safely to Earth – thanks to the commitment, creativity, and teamwork of many people.*

*Lovell was born in 1928 in Parma, Ohio. He lived, for a time, with his mother and with relatives in Terre Haute, Indiana, after his father died in a car accident when the future astronaut was twelve years old. Lovell's love of rocketry took off early; by age ten, he was constructing model rockets. His mother encouraged him to apply to Annapolis, the U.S. Naval Academy, to emulate the path of his uncle, a renowned naval aviator during World War I. Lovell was admitted to the academy on his second attempt. (He completed his first two years of college on an ROTC scholarship at the University of Wisconsin, Madison.) Upon graduation from Annapolis, he joined the U.S. Navy as an aviator.*

*He was accepted into NASA's Space Program in 1962. A recipient of the Presidential Medal of Freedom, Capt. Lovell later launched a successful business career. Today, his calendar remains marked with speaking engagements and similar events. His "office" is located at Lovell's of Lake Forest, a highly reviewed restaurant owned by his son Jay in Chicago's far north suburbs. A history buff, Capt. Lovell's cadre of accomplishments include that of Distinguished Eagle Scout and Silver Buffalo, honors for long-term service to scouting.*

Chicago is my adopted hometown. My grandfather settled here when he emigrated from Czechoslovakia. When my mother was born, the family lived in Oak Park, which had a large Czech community at the time. I was born in Parma, Ohio, but lived there only for the first year of my life.

My participation in the Boy Scouts was a hugely formative experience that influenced my later success. Because my dad died when I was twelve, scouting became my surrogate father. I was on my own a lot. Everything in scouting is mission-oriented and geared to overcoming challenges. Scouting teaches a critical skill that must be learned and acquired, leadership. Leadership leads to strong teamwork, the glue that holds every organization together. During the period when I was trying to obtain my Pathfinder badge, my leader asked me a question to which I didn't know the answer. When I simply told him that I couldn't respond, he replied, "Because you were honest, I will give you credit for it anyway." That experience always stuck with me. When you don't know something, don't try to fake it. Admit it, and move on from there.

My uncle was an important role model. When visiting us, he related great stories of his adventures as a naval aviator. In those days, kids regarded naval aviation in much the same way that today's kids think of space travel – like a fantasy. When I was ten, old enough to understand what aviation *was,* I began reading the work of Robert Goddard, Ph.D., an American physicist and inventor who was the first person to build a liquid-fueled rocket. Rockets grabbed my interest because they represented power and a force that surpassed any other aircraft.

When I applied to be part of the original group of Mercury 7 astronauts in 1958, I was rejected. As it turned out, however, when I was accepted later, in 1962, the timing was even better. The Gemini and Apollo programs were going strong.

Astronauts share common characteristics, and that was especially true in the early days. They were smart people who lived on the edge, loved adventure, and wanted to explore anything new. They are individuals who know how to figure out a plan – and quickly – when something goes wrong.

People often ask me why I didn't react with panic when the situation began deteriorating on Apollo 13. My response? I could have bounced off the walls for ten minutes, but that waste of time would have accomplished nothing. Instead, we asked ourselves, "What do we have on board that could help get us out of this jam?" Everyone's attitude was identical: Let's put our heads together and find a solution.

Once we realized the magnitude of the problems on Apollo 13, all of our efforts were channeled into getting home safely; going to the moon quickly became secondary. But after I returned to earth, disappointment set in. It lasted for about ten years. But when I began writing my book *Lost Moon: The Perilous Voyage of Apollo 13,* I gleaned a better understanding of the experience and all that was accomplished by Mission Control. While the flight itself was not a success, it represented a triumph of how people can manage their way out of a crisis.

If the mission had gone as planned, I would have been the third man to walk on the Moon, but who would remember that? Instead, I overcame near-certain catastrophe and turned it into a successful recovery. That result, ultimately, was more significant to my career than had I actually landed on the Moon.

*Capt. Lovell was interviewed at Lovell's of Lake Forest on September 21, 2012. His birthday is March 25, 1928.*

---

## Favorites

**BOOK**
*The Killer Angels* by Michael Shaara. A current favorite of mine, it's a classic novel of the Civil War.

**MOVIE**
*Master and Commander: The Far Side of the World* (2003), directed by Peter Wier. It's an epic historical drama and seafaring adventure.

**PLACE**
The Adler Planetarium. It brings together all the disciplines I love – astronomy, science, and space flight.

**SONG**
"Ashokan Farewell" by Jay Unger. It's an important part of the *Apollo 13* soundtrack.

**QUOTATION**
"Leadership is the art of getting someone else to do something you want done because he wants to do it."
— PRESIDENT DWIGHT D. EISENHOWER

"*Leadership is the art of...*"

# Ann Lurie

## Philanthropist

Using her good fortune, social conscience, and the memory of her husband, she shares the wealth with those in greatest need.

*A lifelong giver, Ann Lurie and her late husband, Bob, co-founded the Ann and Robert H. Lurie Foundation, a private Chicago-based philanthropic organization, in 1986. A full-time philanthropist, she funds, administers, and – in every sense – leads the charity to which she devotes her time, passions, and commitment. Lurie also is president of Lurie Investments, Inc., which funds her foundation's philanthropy. However, like so many mothers around the globe, she is quick to emphasize that her maternal focus trumps almost every other endeavor. When Bob Lurie passed away in 1990 at age forty-eight, this former pediatric nurse joined the ranks of America's single moms. Her six children were then ages five, seven, nine, eleven, thirteen, and fifteen. Under Lurie's watchful guidance, the foundation has contributed more than $331 million to cancer research, healthcare organizations, food banks, and animal shelters, among other endeavors.*

My childhood was untraditional in that my father literally disappeared from our lives when I was five years old. Wanting to be protective, my mother never said anything negative about him. I never received a good explanation of what happened, so consequently, it's taken me years to come to terms with what was troublesome about my childhood. I'm finally getting a handle on it.

At seventeen, I pulled off a coup that, looking back, was indicative of my later approach to philanthropy. I had a 7:30 a.m. vocabulary class, with a test every Friday. It was difficult for me because I'm not a morning person. After the test was completed, the teacher would distribute the word list for the following week. One day I approached him and said, "As long as I can score an *A* on every test, can you just ignore the fact that I don't attend class on Monday, Tuesday, Wednesday, and Thursday?" To my surprise, he agreed, and I learned that many issues are negotiable if you speak up and then meet the expectations set by yourself and others.

In 2000, when I decided to build a Western-style medical clinic in a remote village in Kenya, a number of people told me that it simply couldn't be done. I replied, "I don't see why not." Early on, I referred to the clinic as "my project" because it was risky from an entrepreneurial standpoint – and I *do* view philanthropic efforts as investments. When the project was deemed unsustainable in late 2012 – and the clinic closed despite all best efforts to obtain additional funding – it was difficult to accept. We tried something nobody had attempted before – to practice Western medicine in the middle of nowhere with no running water, electricity, or sanitary provisions.

Here's how it began: I started visiting Kenya as a safari client. When the business owner learned I was a philanthropist, he asked me to build a nursery school for the children whose parents worked for him. On the first day of school, I looked around at the forty-four Masai kids in the classroom and said, "Oh my God, to one degree or another, most of these kids are sick." I came home from Kenya and started planning the clinic. We employed more than 160 people, more than 50,000 patients were registered, and the clinic's lab ranked as one of the five best in the country.

The medical clinic required the most resources of any project with which I'd ever been involved – time, energy, finances. As with every project, I wanted to know what worked, what didn't work, why it wasn't working, and what I could do to make it work better. Despite the fact that the clinic ultimately closed, a great deal was learned from the initiative that, I hope and trust, will benefit Kenyans in the future.

People need to remember that the dictionary definition of philanthropy is "affection for mankind." It doesn't necessarily involve money. When I was young, my mother encouraged me to do a good deed daily. Following her advice as a teenager gave me a great deal of personal pleasure, and it still feels good. When I walk down Michigan Avenue and see someone looking at a map, I feel compelled to approach and ask if I can help. Ninety percent of people breathe a huge sigh of relief and thank me. I feel as much satisfaction from that action as I do from writing a check.

We all need to start thinking about helping one another in those small kinds of ways. Every problem can't be cured, but let's just keep chipping away – a little bit at a time.

*Ann Lurie was interviewed at the offices of Lurie Investments and the Ann and Robert H. Lurie Foundation in Chicago's River North neighborhood. Her birthday is April 20, 1945.*

## Favorites

**BOOK**

*The Little Prince* by Antoine de Saint-Exupéry. My husband used the book as an analogy for where he thought his soul would be when he died. And indeed, through all the time I knew him, the stars did, in fact, make him laugh!

**MOVIE**

*Bambi* (1942), produced by Walt Disney. I saw this classic as a child and realized that it was possible my mother could die, which terrified me. But everyone who saw the movie felt, and perhaps still feels, compassion for that fawn.

**PLACE**

On the beach in Montecito, California. When I'm there with my two grandchildren, we watch the waves go in and out, which is spiritually and emotionally comforting. The ocean is both predictable and unpredictable. You know there will always be another wave, but you don't know whether it will knock you over or tickle your toes.

**QUOTATION**

"The best thing for being sad, said Merlin, is to learn something. That's the only thing that never fails. . . . You may miss your only love. . . . There is only one thing for it then – to learn."
– T. H. White from *The Once and Future King*

*"There is only one thing for it then – to learn."*

# Martin Marty

## Theologian and Historian

One of America's premier theologians is nurtured daily by the power of his faith.

*Martin E. Marty, Ph.D., is one of the most prominent interpreters of religion and culture today. An American religious scholar with a doctorate from the University of Chicago, he is the author of more than fifty books and has written extensively on eighteenth-, nineteenth-, and twentieth-century American religion. Among the titles are* Righteous Empire: The Protestant Experience in America *and* Accounting for Fundamentalism: The Dynamic Character of Movements. *A former pastor, he taught religious history for thirty-five years at the University of Chicago. The Martin Marty Center at the Divinity School at the University of Chicago is a research center with a special focus on public religion. Marty and his wife, Harriet, live in downtown Chicago. They have six children, nine grandchildren, and four great-grandchildren.*

My father, a Lutheran schoolteacher and church organist, was devoted to J. S. Bach. Thus, Bach was my mother's milk. His music is drenched in spiritual depth. If I waver in my faith or fall into a dark mood, something I am not prone to, I wouldn't run to hear the nearest sermon. Instead, I'd visit a nearby sanctuary, such as the one at Fourth Presbyterian Church, on a Saturday afternoon and listen to the organist practice for the next day's services. That's the root of everything for me.

I was born in West Point, Nebraska [current population 3,400]. My father, Emil, was my upper grades teacher and my inspiration. There's a novel titled *A Simple Honorable Man* by Conrad Richter, which is how I would describe my dad. He educated a great number of the kids in our small town.

The source of my spiritual spark changes little over the years. I practice the Lutheran classical, rather than the conservative, tradition. The catechism says that upon arising in the morning, you should make a sign of the cross as a token of your baptism. There is no yesterday; make amends to anyone you may have offended. My wife accuses me of having no guilt [laughs]. The catechism instructs us to go to our work joyfully. Do the same thing in the evening. Go to sleep cheerfully. The day is past, and there's a new one ahead.

My wife and I sing in the choir at the church we attend regularly. We follow the devotions of the *Daily Texts* of the Moravian Church, which include scripture readings, a New Testament text, a hymn, a prayer, and a psalm.

A 2009 University of Chicago study reported, and I quote, that "Americans' attitudes toward religion are growing more complex. While fewer people identify with a particular religion, belief in God remains high."

The individualization, or privatization, of religion is one of the big stories of our time. Over the past fifty years, the same percentage of people say they believe in God and in heaven and hell. But there have been so many changes in communal life, and this is part of a secular trend.

For example, when you drive into a small town, you often see that the local Moose Lodge and other organizations like it have closed their doors. Plus, there's a great deal that goes on in religious institutions to rebel against. Going to church can be boring; not every church service is stimulating. There are so many choices for people now; they travel, are exposed to all kinds of people, and aren't captive to one set of beliefs.

There are some losses as a result, however. I think of these words of the Apostle Paul: "We are members one of another." The energies amassed by being in community are quite different from what happens when you're on your own spiritual kick. I don't give myself the highest marks on individual prayer, but prayer in community and taking The Lord's Supper are huge for me. When we pray for the twenty people of our parish who are in the military, it means something. I would never pray for these people otherwise. In community, the invisible becomes visible.

*Martin Marty was interviewed on March 23, 2010, in the private library near his downtown Chicago home. It features separate sections on, among other topics, the late eighteenth century, Lutheranism, Catholicism, Americana, reference, theology, and Lutheran pastor and theologian Dietrich Bonhoeffer. His birthday is February 5, 1928.*

## Favorites

**AUTHOR**
Willa Cather. This novelist of the Great Plains speaks to my soul.

**MUSIC**
The works of J. S. Bach, especially the "St. Matthew Passion," the "St. John Passion," and the "Mass in B Minor."

**NONPROFITS**
Opportunity International, which provides small business loans, savings, insurance, and training in basic business practices to people living in poverty, and Habitat for Humanity, a nonprofit, ecumenical Christian organization dedicated to eliminating homelessness worldwide and making affordable shelter a matter of conscience.

**PLACE**
The Nebraska family farm.

**QUOTATION**
"Everything begins in mysticism and ends in politics."
— CHARLES PÉGUY, FRENCH POET

*"Everything begins in mysticism..."*

Lisa Schwartz Photography

# Patricia Monaghan

## Earth Spirituality Writer*

Her love of mythology led to a career that honored the pantheon of wonders served up by the natural world.

*Patricia Monaghan was a professor of interdisciplinary studies at the School for New Learning at DePaul University and she penned more than twenty books, including four volumes of poetry. The work with which Monaghan's name is synonymous is* The Book of Goddesses and Heroines, *which evolved into the two-volume* The Encyclopedia of Goddesses and Heroines. *It has been in print continuously since 1981. Monaghan also wrote lovingly about Celtic traditions, spirituality, folklore, and history. She traveled to Ireland more than thirty times.*

As a young child living in New York, I was so ill with rheumatic fever that I could hardly get out of bed for a few years. I was a great reader and immersed myself in mythology by age ten. The heroic beings were fascinating, as well as sometimes scary and baffling. I was consumed with reading about the female heroines. But I never saw any career possibilities in the study of mythology. Years later, when I taught women's studies, I was surprised to learn my students knew very little about the goddesses. When I sought out a dictionary of goddesses to help educate them, I was amazed to find that one didn't exist. I was thirty years old and naïve about how publishing works, so I decided to write it myself.

I grew up in an era when the Virgin Mary and Marilyn Monroe were the dominant female images – two extremes with little variety in between. What I am proudest about in the goddess encyclopedia is its diversity. More than 10,000 goddesses worldwide are named, and 3,000-plus individual stories are told. Each offers a snapshot of the divine, of the grand mystery of life. Most of us are told that there's one God and one God *only*. An interesting aspect of human history is that every monotheistic religion excludes the feminine – that's why it's important to tell these stories.

The term "earth spirituality" encompasses indigenous and pagan religions that position divinity as existing in the universe, within the cosmos. There's a sense that God is present and eminent everywhere; God is not "out there" somewhere. Paganism recognizes that we are dependent on the earth. We cannot just take; we must also give back. It's not a "woo woo" kind of thing, as many people believe. Rather, pagan rituals celebrate life. On our Wisconsin farm, we have altars around the property and we rejoice in seasonal rituals, such as the harvest. The changing of the seasons is one of the great controlling metaphors of my life.

Because I spent much of my youth in Alaska, the natural world has always represented my source of spiritual strength. My family was Roman Catholic, but even as a small child I related more strongly to nature. I see no difference between a church environment and a "cathedral of the pines." Forty years ago, I became a Quaker. The Society of Friends doesn't distinguish between men and women. The presence of the divine is symbolized by a light – not by a male figurehead.

The fact that I spent many years living in Alaska defines a great deal about me, including the source of my drive and my approach to life. Because Alaska was the last frontier, the lack of pop culture influences and material possessions forged a do-it-yourself attitude. Case in point: a decision to write the goddess book when I discovered that one didn't exist.

I believe everyone should read *The Varieties of Religious Experience* (1902) by philosopher William James, one of our earliest psychologists. It's a crucial book in terms of understanding what different forms of spirituality, and interpretations about them, mean to different groups of people. And no matter what one believes, it's humbling to realize you are just one piece of the mosaic. As James defines it, what I practice is natural mysticism. I'm drenched in it.

*Patricia Monaghan was interviewed at her academic office in Oak Forest, Illinois, on June 14, 2011. She was born on February 15, 1945 and was thrilled to share birthdays with Susan B. Anthony, a leader of the suffragette movement, who was born in 1820.*

★ *Patricia Monaghan died on November 11, 2012, seventeen months after she was interviewed.*

## Favorites

**BOOK**
My compact edition of the *Oxford English Dictionary*.

**NONPROFITS**
Black Earth Institute, a think-tank for artists who connect spirituality, environment, and social justice; Voices from the American Land; and Chicago Wilderness.

**PLACES**
The "Shannon Pot," source of the Shannon River in Ireland; Saint Brigid's Well at Kildare, in Ireland; and our farm in rural Wisconsin.

**PLAY**
*A Midsummer Night's Dream* by William Shakespeare. I have seen it a dozen times, and I could see it a dozen times more.

**POETS**
Arthur Rimbaud, Wallace Stephens, and William Butler Yeats – mystical poets that articulate an inexplicable aspect of the human spiritual experience.

**QUOTATION**
"In dreams begin responsibilities."
– W. B. YEATS, IRISH POET

"*In dreams begin responsibilities.*"

Photo by Renar Photography

# Jim Mullen

## Former Chicago Police Officer, Paralyzed in the Line of Duty

Soaring spirit, abundant humor, and loving family reinforce his vigor – "I am lucky to be alive."

*A cop, particularly an urban one, understands there's no such thing as "an ordinary day." Nobody knows that better than someone like former Chicago Police Officer Jim Mullen. On October 16, 1996, life as he knew it was transformed for the thirty-one-year-old Officer Mullen when he and several other tactical officers responded to a call for help after shots were fired from an apartment building in Rogers Park on Chicago's North Side. During the episode, an off-duty security guard fired a .357 Magnum at the officers. While Mullen dove for cover, a bullet penetrated his cheek, shattering his jaw and piercing his spine. As Chicagoans prayed for his life, Mullen recalls that several of his dear friends were making plans to attend his funeral. After six months of a grueling hospitalization, rehabilitation, and recovery – complete with several surgeries, four heart attacks, and the implantation of a pacemaker – the young family man returned home to his wife, Athena, who had cared for him with such vigilance throughout his ordeal, and his baby daughter, Maggie.*

*Not surprisingly, Mullen has encountered myriad obstacles since the violence that rendered him a quadriplegic who must use a respirator to maintain his breathing. After attempting to return to work with the police department, he launched a foundation (no longer operating) to provide computers for people with disabilities. He then worked for WBBM Channel 2 as a reporter on disability issues, but was laid off. However, a gift from his mom, Audre – in the form of her treasured applesauce recipe – may be infusing Mullen's future with new life. Prepared with all natural ingredients and produced near Rockford, Illinois, Mullen's Chicago's Finest Applesauce is sold to Whole Foods and Jewel, among other local retailers. A portion of the profits benefits the Chicago Police Memorial Foundation. Mullen hopes that geographic distribution of the treat that he devoured as a child may soon be expanded. "It tastes like apple pie without the crust," he smiles.*

My father was a police sergeant on the North Side, as were two of his uncles before him. I used to love to ride with my dad, back in the day when you were allowed to do that. Many of my parents' friends were cops, and we all kind of flocked together. I grew up knowing I would become a police officer, even though I worked in the private sector for a while. I loved everything about a cop's life, especially the humor and the satisfaction of putting bad guys in jail. I spent my entire law enforcement career in Rogers Park, a great district because it's so culturally diverse.

I think of myself as just a regular guy, even though many people call me a hero. What I experienced on the day of the shooting might have been "heroic," but that's not the same thing. There were six other tactical officers at the scene, and they risked their lives every bit as much as I did. Cops endanger themselves every day; that's what the job is about.

After I was shot, the odds of survival were against me. My wife, Athena, stayed with me all day, and my parents took the night shift. I was never alone. Athena taped a picture of our baby daughter to the ceiling above my head to inspire me. The late Cardinal Bernadin, although he was gravely ill, visited me in the hospital. I believe that because of him, in part, thousands of Chicagoans actively prayed for me. Many still do so today. You often hear people say that everything happens for a reason, but I'm not sure I believe that's true.

After I spent more than two months in a medically induced coma and finally awoke, the medical staff gave me a communications board to spell out, with letters and pictures, what I wanted to say. Typically, my first comment was a joke. I spelled out "cheap seats" because my hospital bed was located right next to the door of the intensive care unit.

The aftermath of the accident has been more difficult for my wife and my family than for me. Quite frankly, I am a realist. I was shot in the right cheek with a .357 Magnum. The very idea that I am still alive is incredible. I am not bitter towards the man who shot me. [Note: The shooter died in prison in 2011.] Some days, yes, I'm angry. However, you need to forgive so that you can keep moving forward. Athena and I try to keep things simple, but the responsibilities I have as a husband, son, and father are still there. It's been a tough road. When you become paralyzed, learning how to care for yourself becomes your full-time job. However, I am fortunate to have access to the best medical care and resources, ones which many others might not have available.

I want people to understand that there is life after paralysis, and it can be a wonderful life. Your life isn't over, but it *is* more difficult. I am happy about many things, including a wonderful family and many good friends. One pleasure that I most enjoy is sitting in the passenger seat of my blue 1970 Oldsmobile convertible and taking a ride up Sheridan Road with the top down. I really am the same old guy I used to be, I just don't move as quickly.

*Jim Mullen was interviewed at his home on Chicago's Northwest Side on August 29, 2012. His birthday is May 3, 1964.*

---

## Favorites

**MOVIES**
*Caddy Shack* (1980), directed by Harold Ramis; *The Blues Brothers* (1980), directed by John Landis; and *The Quiet Man* (1952), directed by John Ford. These were the ones I loved to watch when I was growing up.

**NONPROFIT**
Chicago Police Memorial Foundation. This important organization supports and assists the families of Chicago Police Officers who were killed or catastrophically injured in the line of duty.

**PLACE**
Diversey Harbor. I always feel hopeful there, probably because I spent many summer nights there as a kid.

**QUOTATION**
"People sleep peaceably in their beds at night only because rough men stand ready to do violence on their behalf."

— GEORGE ORWELL, BRITISH WRITER OF DYSTOPIAN CLASSICS

*"only because rough men stand ready..."*

# Elise Paschen

## Poet and Poetry Advocate

This writer changes lives through an art form that is heart-stopping, laughter-inducing, and capable of evoking tears.

*Chicago poet Elise Paschen, D.Phil., is a self-described "poetry advocate." She spreads that fervor with creativity, imagination, and enthusiasm. The latest of her three volumes of poetry is* Bestiary. *Paschen co-founded Poetry in Motion (launched in 1992 and still ongoing), a program that places poetry placards in buses and subways in selected cities. The daughter of prima ballerina Maria Tallchief, co-founder of the Chicago City Ballet, and Chicago builder Henry Paschen, she is of Osage descent. She coedited the bestselling anthology,* Poetry Speaks (now Poetry Speaks Expanded: Hear Poets Read Their Own Work from Tennyson to Plath). *The popularity of the book inspired the subsequent titles* Poetry Speaks to Children *and, for adolescents,* Poetry Speaks Who I Am: Poems of Discovery, Inspiration, Independence, and Everything Else. *Paschen attended Chicago's Francis W. Parker School and Harvard University and holds M.Phil. and D.Phil degrees in Twentieth Century British and American Literature from Oxford University.*

In third grade, when I received a copy of the *Oxford Book of Poetry for Children*, I fell in love with William Blake's poem "The Tyger." There's something spiritual about the cadence and the force of "The Tyger," and it gave me great power to memorize and recite it. ["Tyger! Tyger! burning bright, in the forest of the night. What immortal hand or eye could frame thy fearful symmetry?"] Poetry provided a way for me to navigate into the world of writing.

Growing up, I always knew that I would choose a career and be passionate about it. After all, I was a backstage baby. My mother, a world-renowned prima ballerina, was devoted to her art and she was a great influence on my life. In college, I became serious about writing poetry, especially after my professor, Seamus Heaney, urged me to read the manuscripts of William Butler Yeats. Through studying his drafts, I learned the importance of revising, again and again, until the work is right.

Poems are life changing. Poetry matters because it condenses reality into a short amount of time and space. It's visceral in a way that makes your heart stop, makes you laugh, and makes you cry. During my time as executive director of the Poetry Society of America, we launched *Poetry in Motion,* which features posters of poems of 16 lines or fewer in buses and subways. The goal is to grab people's attention in the midst of their busy days by reaching them at an emotional level. Poetry is an inspiring way to connect with young people. When I worked on the anthology *Poetry Speaks to Children,* my son began to dance when I played a recording of a Tolkien poem. Poetry also can help older kids understand and express the emotions and isolation that they may experience as teenagers.

Many of my poems are inspired by the natural world, as well as human nature. In Chicago, a place that moves me is the Magic Hedge, a 150-yard stretch of shrubs and trees in the Montrose Point Bird Sanctuary. There's a strange juxtaposition in how it teems with wildlife, discovery, and a sense of danger.

One of my favorite poems from *Poetry in Motion* is "Magic Words" by an anonymous Inuit poet, translated by Edward Field, describing the powerful connection between the human and animal worlds. As a writer, you must make a willful decision to turn everything off and learn how to isolate, concentrate, and spend a great deal of time creating your own inner space, a place from which you can write.

My early Catholic upbringing, I'm sure, has affected my writing and my sense of the world. When I received my first communion at Holy Name Cathedral, the nuns told my mother I was very spiritual and may even have a calling! When the time for confirmation approached, my mother told me that I should choose whether to be confirmed or not. I decided not to, and in some ways, that decision has weighed on me. I've written about the experience in my poem "Confirmation." I've grappled with not "advancing" in the religion – not going to confession or taking communion in a Catholic church. My husband and I married in a small Methodist country church in Martha's Vineyard, Massachusetts, and later baptized our children at Kenilworth Union Church. Our children and I say our prayers every night, but we attend church, at St. Clement Catholic Church in Chicago, only on Easter and Christmas.

I am proud of being one-quarter Osage Indian. We return as often as possible to visit Oklahoma, where my mother lived in a yellow brick house on a hill overlooking a field. We have many relatives there. I take my children with me so they'll be more aware of our heritage. My mother grew up in Beverly Hills, so she did not have many memories of Osage customs and beliefs. I wish she'd had more memories to share. I was honored when Molly Peacock wrote about *Bestiary*: "One feels Paschen's Osage roots in these poems where she makes the deepest emotions palpable through her stunning craft."

*Elise Paschen was interviewed at her home in the Lincoln Park neighborhood on June 28, 2010. She was born on January 4, 1959.*

## Favorites

**BOOK**
*Love in the Time of Cholera* by Gabriel García Márquez.

**MOVIE**
*Notorious* (1946), directed by Alfred Hitchcock. In this brilliant allegory of love and betrayal, Hitchcock fuses two of his favorite elements: suspense and romance.

**MUSIC**
"Prelude to the Afternoon of a Faun" by French composer Claude Debussy.

**PLAY**
*King Lear* by William Shakespeare.

**POET**
William Butler Yeats, an Irish poet and one of the foremost figures of twentieth century literature.

**POET FOR SPIRITUAL INSPIRATION**
Gerard Manley Hopkins, one of the Victorian era's greatest poets.

**POET I'M READING NOW**
Edward Hirsch, a Chicago-born poet who also wrote *How to Read a Poem and Fall in Love with Poetry*.

**QUOTATION**
"There is no separation between poetry, the stories and events that link them, or the music that holds it all together, just as there is no separation between human, animal, plant, sky, and earth . . ."
– POET JOY HARJO OF THE MYSKOKE/CREEK NATION

"*There is no separation...*"

# Eboo Patel

## Founder and President, Interfaith Youth Core

Nurturing a movement that is changing outmoded models of divisiveness among diverse religious groups, the organization's creed is: "Better together."

*Eboo Patel, Ph.D., is the founder and president of Interfaith Youth Core (IFYC), a Chicago-based nonprofit building the global interfaith youth movement. He authored a memoir,* Acts of Faith: The Story of an American Muslim, the Struggle for the Soul of a Generation, *and* Sacred Ground: Pluralism, Prejudice and the Promise of America. *The former is required reading on 11 college campuses, according to a 2011 article in* The New York Times. *Patel has spoken about his vision at venues such as a TED Conference, the Clinton Global Initiative, and the Nobel Peace Prize Forum.*

*He served on President Obama's inaugural Advisory Council of the White House Office of Faith-Based and Neighborhood Partnerships. Describing Eboo Patel, Joshua DuBois, former executive director of the White House Office of Faith-Based and Neighborhood Partnerships, said in an interview with* The New York Times, *"You have people who can cast a vision but then not implement the vision. Then you have people who are great implementers but are not very inspirational. Eboo is a unique leader who can do both."*

*Patel grew up in Glen Ellyn, Illinois. As an undergraduate, he attended the University of Illinois at Urbana-Champaign and earned a degree in sociology. He holds a doctorate in the sociology of religion from Oxford University, where he studied on a Rhodes scholarship.*

Growing up, we were religious in the way many American families are religious: It was important, but we didn't always make it to Friday prayers. American life is so challenging and achievement-oriented: School, work, and other commitments often interfered. But Islam was always in the air, and we followed its traditions and beliefs. We never ate pork, and we always said *Bismillah*, a blessing meaning "in the name of God," before a meal or leaving the house.

However, I didn't own the religion for myself until I re-engaged with it through two paths – social justice and diversity – as a college student at the University of Illinois. I realized that most of my heroes – Martin Luther King, Jr., Gandhi, Dorothy Day, and others – were motivated to undertake their work through their faith. I'd encountered people from many faiths over my life, and those experiences were powerful in making me ask questions about my own faith.

When I was a teenager, my best friends were a Jew, a Hindu, an Evangelical, a Mormon, a Catholic, and a Lutheran. We never discussed religion; it just wasn't part of public conversation. One day a group of thugs in my high school beat up my Jewish friend. I just stood by while it happened, and I was silent. Years later, my dad told me that by failing to intervene, I had not live up to Islamic teachings. He made me ask myself, 'What is it about Islam that requires me to stand up for a person of another faith?' In my early twenties, I learned that my grandmother provided shelter to abused women. When I asked her why she did this, she told me that it was part of the Muslim tradition. These two experiences led me to a serious study of Islam through the pursuit of a doctorate in the sociology of religion at Oxford.

One of my heroes is Hull House Founder Jane Addams. She was inspired by something cosmic to build a remarkable institution. Hull House engaged one of the greatest challenges of its time: How could we successfully integrate a large group of immigrants? The meaning of her work is that every newcomer to America should be viewed as an equal at the table. Part of America's greatness rests on its ability to invite the talents of people from the four corners of the earth.

That same thinking applies to the Interfaith Youth Core. We're addressing one of the most significant issues of *our* time: How will people of different religious backgrounds get along with each other? The IFYC seeks to be an institution that offers a vision of a country where people from different backgrounds are engaged in understanding and cooperation in a world that sees images of religious conflict every day. I now meet with people like President Obama, which would have been unthinkable a decade ago.

It likely will take thirty years to make interfaith cooperation a social norm – much like environmentalism. I am a small player in a far larger plan.

*Eboo Patel was interviewed on February 26, 2010, at the former offices of the Interfaith Youth Core in Chicago's Greektown neighborhood. His birthday is February 9, 1975.*

## Favorites

**MOVIE**
*The Princess Bride* (1987), directed by Rob Reiner. This version of a classic fairy tale is complete with giants, an evil prince, and a beautiful princess.

**MUSIC**
The Grateful Dead and Wilco.

**NONPROFITS**
Teach for America, which aims to end educational inequity; Harlem Children's Zone, a community-based organization in New York City offering education, social services, and community-building programs; and Ashoka, a global association of the world's leading social entrepreneurs.

**PLACE**
Muir Woods in San Francisco. I stand there to pay homage to John Muir, who built the environmental movement in America.

**PLAY**
*Angels in America.* This Tony Kushner play melds love, hate, religion, and politics into a uniquely American epic.

**POET**
Rumi, a Persian poet of the thirteenth century. I fell in love with him before I even realized he was a Muslim and that everything he communicates comes from Islam. He represents shockingly open universal love.

**QUOTATION**
"Your job is to move the world a millionth of an inch."
— GARY SNYDER, BUDDHIST POET

"*...move the world a millionth of an inch.*"

# Rachel Barton Pine

## Virtuoso Violinist

After captivating her at age three, music has suffused this Chicagoan's life in pleasure, drama, and aspirations fulfilled.

*Rachel Barton Pine is one of the world's most beloved violinists. Born and raised in Chicago's North Center neighborhood, she won her first competition at age seven and joined the Civic Orchestra of Chicago at age twelve. Pine won a gold medal in the J. S. Bach International Violin Competition in Leipzig, Germany, at age seventeen. She is away from home more than half the days of the year in performance around the world, usually traveling with her husband, Greg Pine. The violin she plays at most of her concerts is the "ex-Soldat," made in 1742 by Joseph Guarneri "del Gesu."*

*About her playing, the* Chicago Tribune *lauded: "Few can play as beautifully as Barton . . . the commanding ease with which she applied fingers and horsehair to the breathless roulades and passage work was enough to put the crowd in her thrall, as if they weren't fans already." The* All Music Guide *proclaims: "Rachel Barton Pine really may be the most charismatic, the most virtuosic, and the most compelling American violinist of her generation."*

When I was three years old, I attended a service at our family church, Saint Pauls United Church of Christ in Lincoln Park. A few middle-school-aged girls, wearing beautiful long dresses, were playing the violin. I stood up in the pew, pointed to the girls, and declared, "I want to do that!" I began lessons soon after that time, and at age four, I played my first Bach solo at church.

There was a stained glass window of J. S. Bach in the sanctuary and, when I was very young, I thought Bach ranked right up there with the guys from the Bible – God, Jesus, and Bach – and not necessarily in that order [laughs]. I grew up understanding that the purpose of music was to lift the human spirit and bring us closer to God. Because I began by playing in church, I've never experienced stage fright. We're all in this together. I am there to share my music, and the audience – whoever they may be – is there to be caught up in it.

My mom often encouraged me to put away my violin and go outside to play. I remember when she realized that the violin would be my life. At age five, my school took a group of us children to visit a nursing home to sing and play instruments. As I approached one room, alone, a nurse took me aside to explain that the man I was about to play for had not spoken in years, even though he knew how to talk. She wanted to make me feel comfortable knowing that I would elicit no reaction. But after I played, the man cried and told me about how he, too, had played the violin. It was extraordinary.

My solo debut was at age seven. My family already was experiencing financial difficulties. Our electricity was often turned off, the rent was frequently late, and my practice room was unheated. Home schooling, starting at age eight, saved my life. In addition to my academics, I could practice as many hours as needed – eight hours a day by age eleven, plus lessons and coaching.

Scholarships covered music lessons, but my instruments were borrowed and my performance dresses came from thrift shops. At fourteen, I began contributing substantially to the family's finances. Our situation was so dramatic that my mother bought discounted fruits. She carved out the bad parts and salvaged what remained. I felt fortunate to help bring stability to the family through my music.

At age twenty, I was severely injured and nearly lost my life when I was caught in the door of a commuter train and dragged. However, I don't consider it to have been a turning point in my life, never asking, "Why did God let this happen to me?" or "Did God do this to me for a reason?" Rather, I subscribe to the dumb-luck theory: Although I experienced something horrible, I also was extremely fortunate that there were two men at the scene who knew how to craft a tourniquet – the action that saved my life. I believe in God's loving presence in both good and bad times.

Here's my advice for achieving the most from your life: Figure out who you are, identify the ultimate gift that you can offer, and discover where these two things align. Work as hard as you can. Remember that you must possess blind faith when you can't see where the path is leading you. Keep striving as if you know where you're headed.

*Rachel Barton Pine was interviewed at her home in Chicago's River North neighborhood on March 30, 2011. Her birthday is October 11, 1974.*

# Favorites

**BOOKS**
*The Song of the Lioness* by Tamora Pierce. This series of young adult fantasy novels published in the 1980s features a red-haired girl as the main character. She dresses as a boy so she can become a knight.

**MOVIE**
*Farinelli* (1994), directed by Gérard Corbiau. This biographical story details the life and career of the Italian opera singer Farinelli, considered one of the greatest castrato performers of all time.

**NONPROFIT**
The Rachel Elizabeth Barton Foundation. Expanding awareness of and appreciation for classical music, the organization provides services and funding for classical music education, research, performances, and artists, to benefit listeners and learners alike.

**PERFORMER**
Maud Powell (1867-1920). The first American-born violinist to receive international renown, she was the greatest American violinist of either gender.

**QUOTATION**
"We are not given to know what might have been."
— C. S. LEWIS, BRITISH WRITER, ACADEMIC, AND LAY THEOLOGIAN

"*We are not given to know...*"

# Stephen Ross

## Primatologist and Animal Welfare Specialist, Lincoln Park Zoo

A champion of chimpanzees, he forged a bond with the species at age seven – long before he ever laid eyes on one.

*Stephen Ross, Ph.D., Director, Lester E. Fisher Center for the Study and Conservation of Apes at Lincoln Park Zoo, joined the zoo staff in 2000 as a behavior specialist. He played a leadership role in the design of the award-winning Regenstein Center for African Apes, which opened in 2004. Previously, Ross held a variety of positions in animal research with various species, including a job as lead research specialist at Yerkes Regional Primate Center at Emory University, Atlanta. His expertise focuses on chimpanzee behavior, comparative ape cognition, and animal welfare. Ross co-edited the recently published* The Mind of the Chimpanzee. *Academic credentials include a B.Sc. in zoology from the University of Guelph, Ontario, Canada; an M.A. in social science from the University of Chicago; and a Ph.D. (Department of Experimental Medicine) from the University of Copenhagen in Denmark.*

At about age seven, I saw a television program that started everything – perhaps a National Geographic episode on primatologist Jane Goodall. From an early age, I was fascinated with the similarity between apes and humans. As a result of Jane's research, anthropomorphizing [attributing human form or personality to things not human] became more acceptable because it was clear that chimps feel and behave much as humans do. Through my early school years, I read as many books as I could find on chimps. My parents had no background in animals or zoology. If they were skeptical about my dream of working with chimps, they never let on.

My interest in animal welfare began in high school as an emotional connection. With a natural ability in math and science, it occurred to me that I could combine what I'd thought of as two quite separate interests into one career – as an animal welfare scientist. By a somewhat strategic approach of taking a series of jobs not directly related to my area of interest, chimps, I was fortunate to be hired in my current role.

I have the best job in the world. Lincoln Park Zoo is considered a small to medium sized facility, but it's one of the country's top three zoos in terms of its reputation for conservation and scientific research. Free admission is another huge plus.

The statistic that we share approximately 98.5 percent of our DNA with chimps can be misleading. We also share 88 percent of our DNA with dandelions. The more important fact is that chimpanzees are more similar to humans genetically than they are to gorillas. One thing I find most interesting is observing chimps' faults as a species. Learning how violent and how awful they can be to one another hasn't lessened my admiration for them because we see exactly the same faults in humans. I also see their great ability to be gentle and affectionate. I often hear people criticize the tendency of chimps to be aggressive, but really, humans are the last ones who should be throwing stones.

Two of my favorite nonprofit organizations are committed to the protection of chimpanzees. The first is Chimp Haven, a national sanctuary that provides lifetime care of chimpanzees that have been retired from medical research or are no longer wanted as pets. Private chimp ownership is a practice that virtually all primatologists decry. The second organization is Project ChimpCare, which gathers information about where chimps live and how they are cared for. Enlarging this information base is essential to providing data to ensure these animals are cared for in the future. [Note: Stephen Ross founded this organization in 2002.]

Animal welfare is a weird confluence of emotion and science. I want to make animals happy. By measuring their welfare, as a scientist, and then determining how to improve it, I experience an emotional connection to these animals, which has become my spiritual source.

*Stephen Ross was interviewed on April 28, 2011 at the Regenstein Center for the Apes at Lincoln Park Zoo. His birthday is December 16, 1969.*

## Favorites

**BOOK ABOUT CHIMPANZEES**

*Chimpanzee Politics: Power and Sex Among Apes* by Dutch primatologist Frans de Waal. A longtime student of simian behavior, de Waal analyzes the behavior of a captive tribe of chimpanzees, comparing its actions with those of ape societies.

**MOVIE**

*Memento* (2000), directed by Christopher Nolan. A psychological thriller, it was cool, innovative, and unexpected.

**QUOTATION**

"We need another and a wiser and perhaps a more mystical concept of animals. They are not brethren, they are not underlings, they are other nations, caught with ourselves in the net of life and time, fellow prisoners of the splendor and travail of the earth."
– HENRY BESTON, AMERICAN WRITER AND NATURALIST, FROM *THE OUTERMOST HOUSE: A YEAR OF LIFE ON THE GREAT BEACH OF CAPE COD*

"*...a more mystical concept of animals.*"

# Janet Rowley

## Cancer Genetics Pioneer*

"Once I knew I was right about my discovery, I did not care who thought I was wrong," recalls this Presidential Medal of Freedom honoree.

*Eighty-seven years old when we spoke in January 2012, Janet Rowley, M.D., continued working part-time in her laboratory at the University of Chicago. She was the Blum-Riese Distinguished Service Professor. At that late stage in her life, Rowley's primary objective was to help others, particularly younger research scientists – just as she was supported by more established peers before making a revolutionary breakthrough in 1972. At that time, she identified a chromosomal translocation (the exchange of genetic material between chromosomes in patients with leukemia) as the cause of leukemia and other cancers.*

*Rowley's discovery, followed by her subsequent contributions on recurring chromosomal abnormalities, proved that some cancers are clearly genetic in nature – opening the door to new prevention and treatment methods.*

*Born in New York City and raised on Chicago's South Side, Rowley's academic prowess surfaced early. In 1940, at age fifteen, she was one of an intellectually elite group provided with full scholarships to study at the University of Chicago Four-Year-College developed by Robert M. Hutchins, then president of the University of Chicago. The innovative program married the last two years of high school with the first two years of college. Rowley later earned her Bachelor of Science and Doctor of Medicine degrees from the University of Chicago.*

Both of my parents were University of Chicago graduates, and I always was encouraged to excel at academics. In 1944, as a pre-med major at age nineteen, I applied to medical school at the University of Chicago, but the quota for women students – three out of a class of sixty-five – was filled. I was not angry; it is just the way things were back then. I was admitted the following year, and I married my husband, Donald, a research pathologist, immediately after graduation in 1948.

In 1959, during a period when I worked in a clinic treating patients with mental retardation at Cook County Hospital, now John H. Stroger, Jr. Hospital of Cook County, an important discovery was made about the cause of Down Syndrome – that it was a chromosomal disorder that results in an extra copy of chromosome 21. Soon after that discovery, as luck would have it, my husband took a sabbatical at Oxford University in London. I found there an opportunity to study in a lab working on the emerging field of cytogenetics, a branch of genetics focused on the study of the structure and function of the chromosomes, the carriers of genetic material in the cell.

When we returned to Chicago, thanks to a University of Chicago professor who granted me lab space, I was able to continue a project I'd begun in England. Through him, I obtained access to a microscope and a darkroom, and I got paid. The most difficult challenge facing me was childcare. Our fourth son was born in 1963. Because I was the mother of young children and worked only three half days a week, I needed a housekeeper only on a limited basis. Most housekeepers, understandably, sought full-time positions. I went through four housekeepers in eight weeks, and it was a mess. I finally found one who stayed with us for twenty years; if I hadn't done so, I'm certain I would have given up at some point.

A few years after I began studying patients with all types of leukemia, a new research technique (banding) was developed in England that eventually helped lead to my discovery that the chromosomal abnormality in Chronic Myelogenous Leukemia (CML) patients *wasn't a result of missing genetic material, but rather, the cause of it.*

I remember experiencing a eureka moment right at my dining room table. I worked from photographs of chromosomes, which I would then cut out and put together, like a puzzle, right on the table. In that aha moment, I observed something I had seen only once before; a known chromosome abnormality in CML was not missing a piece, as had been thought, but the "missing piece" had been moved to another chromosome – a translocation.

There was some resistance to my discovery within the scientific community. Many people thought, "Who is *she* to question established scientific thinking?" Nearly a decade passed before my finding was fully accepted. The final step occurred when the World Health Organization acknowledged it. However, if I hadn't made this discovery, someone else would have looked through a microscope and recognized the same abnormality. I truly believe that most people don't give luck enough credit. It plays an enormous role in all of our lives.

Because I received the National Medal of Science in 1999, I was surprised to be honored with the Presidential Medal of Freedom in 2009. It was wonderful to have my husband, four children, and five grandchildren all there together in the East Room of the White House with President Obama. So much good has happened to me. I just want to give back to others for as long as I can.

*Janet Rowley was interviewed on January 11, 2012, in the living room of her Hyde Park home. She was born on April 5, 1925.*

★ *Janet Rowley died on December 17, 2013, twenty-three months after she was interviewed for this book.*

## Favorites

**BOOK ABOUT CANCER**
*The Emperor of All Maladies: A Biography of Cancer,* by Siddhartha Mukherjee, which won the 2011 Pulitzer Prize for General Nonfiction. The jury described it as "an elegant inquiry, at once clinical and personal."

**BOOKS**
As a child, I loved reading stories about girls who were quite determined, such as *Heidi, Anne of Green Gables,* and *Anne of Avonlea.*

**MOVIE**
*It Happened One Night* (1934), a classic directed by Frank Capra. It's so romantic.

**MUSIC**
I love Cole Porter. You really have to pay attention to understand the lyrics, which are clever and original.

**NONPROFIT**
The Nature Conservancy. Mankind is destroying the earth; organizations that strive to protect our planet are important.

**QUOTATIONS**
My grandmother's aphorisms, such as "He who wastes shall surely come to want" and "Handsome is as handsome does."

"*He who wastes shall surely come to want.*"

# Tim Samuelson

## Cultural Historian, City of Chicago

Pulsing through his veins is the very lifeblood of the city itself, from the seedy to the sensational to the sublime.

*You can immerse yourself in Chicago's storied past while visiting the office of the City of Chicago's cultural historian – a position that was created just for him in 2002. Tim Samuelson's walls are bedecked with drawings, illustrations, and photos of Chicago's architectural icons. A credenza displays mementos from gone-but-never-forgotten buildings – including a piece of an echo chamber from the original Chess Records studio on Chicago's South Side. (That's where giants like Bo Diddley, Chuck Berry, and the Rolling Stones expressed their own brands of joyful noise.)*

*Samuelson delights in telling visitors that his city office is the only such workspace housing a player piano. Formerly, he was a preservation specialist at the Chicago Landmarks Commission and Curator of Architecture at the Chicago Historical Society, now the Chicago History Museum.*

At age seven, while visiting my grandmother and looking through the *Reader's Digest*, I saw a drawing of the Carson Pirie Scott Building, designed by Louis Sullivan, and one of the Robie House, designed by Frank Lloyd Wright. Right then, I asked my grandmother if she'd take me to Carson's on her next visit there. I'll never forget my introduction to this building. There was such amazing power and energy present. Then, I goaded my dad into taking me down to the Robie House at the University of Chicago campus.

I was consumed with strange historical things from a very young age. My classmates were nice, but we didn't have much in common. As a result, historical figures became my imaginary friends.

Truthfully, my parents were perplexed and even a bit concerned about my obsession with Chicago history. When I was a teenager, my dad's exact words were, "This is all well and good, son, but what are you going to do about getting a real job?" My dad worked in printing and he'd arranged an internship for me, which I declined. I know that his feelings were hurt, but I just continued on my merry way, followed my instincts, and never let anything stop me. I've created jobs for myself based on my belief in what's interesting and important about Chicago.

I want to convey the essence of Chicago's spirit and give a voice to the amazing people who created the city but are no longer here.

I've always felt there was some kind of underlying presence or energy in things from long ago. From a practical standpoint, even as a kid, I realized there wasn't anything "magical" going on. I peacefully coexist with these ideas, but I don't think or talk about it too much because I might end up spoiling the magic. I kind of feel some buildings are alive. Of course, I know better [laughs], but sometimes I give my favorite buildings a little pat [taps his desk three times] as I pass by.

One of Chicago's great themes is to be passionate about what you want to do, put your own spin on it, and then act. It's a highly creative city that attracts many people with unconventional ideas. From the start of Chicago's history, it was different from the East Coast. The big cities there, like New York and Philadelphia, had long-established ideas on how things should be done. Chicago attracted outsiders who – if they had the chutzpah and energy to pull off new ideas – could do so here. Chicago didn't actively encourage this kind of thing; rather, there was nobody here to tell you not to try something. Look at Louis Sullivan, for example. He taught skyscrapers how to soar.

Sullivan's entire philosophy is that human beings are part of the natural world, but they possess gifts of thinking, reason, and creativity. This idea resonates with me: Each individual has, within himself, the power to draw upon his time, place, and circumstances to creatively express himself through whatever endeavor he chooses.

The real secret in life is to keep your mind open and let things find you. Don't be afraid to explore and wonder about things that come your way. History is my calling. One of my grammar school teachers remarked on a report card that I was too much of a dreamer. I'm still a dreamer, but now I use that enthusiasm to bring others aboard and help them claim history for themselves.

*Tim Samuelson was interviewed on August 10, 2011, at his Cultural Center office at 72 East Randolph Street, Chicago. His birthday is June 16, 1951.*

## Favorites

**BOOK**

*Autobiography of an Idea* by Louis Sullivan. The focus is on his development as a creative human being.

**PLACE**

Lawrence's Fisheries, 2120 South Canal Street, right on the Chicago River. When I'm feeling down, I go there and buy a little bag of fried shrimp. Then I sit on the dock amidst the old factories with the bridges going up and down and the train whistles blowing.

**POET**

Nicholas Vachel Lindsay. A poet born in Springfield, Illinois, he's known as the father of modern "singing poetry."

**SONG**

"Solace" by Scott Joplin. It breaks me up when I listen to it.

**QUOTATION**

"Whenever A annoys or injures B on the pretense of saving or improving X, A is a scoundrel."
— H. L. MENCKEN, TWENTIETH-CENTURY JOURNALIST AND SOCIAL CRITIC

"*the pretense of saving or improving...*"

# Barbara Schermer

## Astrologer

She considers it a sacred experience to interpret a chart: "Souls are revealed."

*A practicing astrologer for thirty years, Barbara Schermer has conducted more than 20,000 consultations for individual and corporate clients from as far away as China and Australia. She is the author of* Astrology Alive! A Guide to Experiential Astrology and the Healing Arts. *Schermer twice has been nominated for the prestigious Regulus Award, presented at the annual United Astrology Conference, for her contributions to astrology. In choosing an astrologer, she recommends seeking strengths in four areas: technical competence, interpretive skill, counseling ability, and ethical standards. Schermer trained for twelve years at the Temple of Kriya Yoga in Chicago, studying astrology, yoga, and the development of consciousness. She now resides near Guadalajara, Mexico. Many of her consultations take place on the telephone.*

In 1973, I attended, unexpectedly, an advanced class in astrology at the Temple of Kriya Yoga in Chicago's Logan Square neighborhood. When I walked into the room, I heard the language of astrology as something that was very familiar. I soon began studying basic astrology with Sri Goswami Kriyananda, who became my guru. [Note: Sri Goswami Kriyananda is the Spiritual Preceptor of the Temple of Kriya Yoga.]

I think of astrology as a language of the psyche, which is how Carl Jung described it. When I hear people say, "I don't believe in astrology," I think that's like saying, "I don't believe in Spanish." That attitude comes from misinformation and from the triviality of horoscopes that appear in daily newspaper columns, which are nonsense. I've told many people that they will never regret studying astrology. It helps in developing an understanding of yourself, the important people in your life, and in deciphering what is unfolding ahead of you. It's also a way to look back on past events with a more detached perspective.

As a child, I attended a Protestant church. I wasn't overly religious, but I grew up with a spiritual respect. At four years old I experienced a spiritual turning point when my brother, who had lumbar polio, was only two hours away from being put in an iron lung. My parents prayed for a long time, and they felt his recovery was a miracle. Every Tuesday, after my brother recovered, we had a half-hour of prayer time as a family. I learned to value contemplation and to love silence at a young age. I found my true spiritual self in 1973 when I met Goswami Kriyananda and was initiated into Kriya Yoga. It is based on the Shankya Yoga philosophy that from the one comes the two – the masculine and the feminine qualities of life.

When on vacation in Saugatuck, Michigan, at age ten, I saw the deep night sky for the first time. I dropped to my knees; it was a mysterious and holy experience for me.

The source of my spiritual spark includes many practices: my Kriya Yoga lineage; two "initiations" with the Dalai Lama, focused on specific spiritual rituals to open up particular energy channels and on how energy and consciousness stream through your body; vision quests, a rite of passage intended to help participants receive guidance from the spirit world, with the Lakota Sioux; and leadership and participation in approximately sixty sweat lodges. I also walk a medicine wheel in my yard. The primary technique I use is mantra chanting – sacred sound – an active meditative process that helps me stay focused.

I consider it a sacred experience to interpret a chart. My role is to illuminate the language of astrology, its symbols and archetypes, and then to communicate the meaning back as simply as I can. My clients don't realize it, but when I offer insight into their charts, they show me their souls. I feel honored to be a witness to their lives.

*Barbara Schermer was interviewed by telephone on March 9, 2011. Her birthday is June 15, 1947.*

---

## Favorites

**ASTROLOGY BOOK**
*The Book of Life: How to Live Life According to the Heavens* by Renaissance astrologer Marsilio Ficino.

**BOOK**
*Autobiography of a Yogi* by Paramhansa Yogananda.

**MOVIE**
*There's Something About Mary* (1998), directed by Bobby and Peter Farrelly. It's simply hilarious.

**MUSIC**
"The Four Seasons" by Italian composer Antonio Vivaldi, a set of violin concertos composed in 1723.

**NONPROFIT**
Alliance for the Great Lakes. Through policy, education, and local efforts, the organization aims to preserve the Great Lakes Region – the world's largest freshwater resource – as a national treasure.

**PLACE**
Chicago's Graceland Cemetery on the city's North Side. When I walk to Daniel Burnham's island, I thank him for preserving Chicago's lakefront and keeping it free and clear for the public.

**QUOTATION**
"Ah, not to be cut off, not through the slightest partition shut out from the law of the stars. The inner – what is it – if not intensified sky, hurled through with birds and deep with the winds of homecoming."
– RAINER MARIE RILKE, GERMAN POET, FROM *AHEAD OF ALL PARTING, THE SELECTED POETRY AND PROSE*

*"...deep with the winds of homecoming."*

# Paul Sereno

Paleontologist and
"Dinosaur Hunter"

Chicago's own Indiana Jones, this renowned
explorer of dinosaur domains thrills at sharing
science's allure with local underserved youth.

*A National Geographic Society explorer-in-residence and professor of paleontology, evolution, and anatomy at the University of Chicago, Paul Sereno, Ph.D., is leaving an indelible imprint on the field of paleontology, the study of prehistory. Over the course of twenty expeditions, he has uncovered several new dinosaur species in locations as far-flung as Niger, Morocco, Argentina, and Inner Mongolia. Sereno's fascination with the natural world surfaced early – when he and his brother transformed the gift of a simple butterfly kit into a mini laboratory that grew and nurtured moths. He holds a B.S. in biological sciences from Northern Illinois University and an M.A. in vertebrate paleontology, an M.Phil. in geological sciences and a Ph.D. in geological sciences from Columbia University, New York. One of Sereno's most publicized discoveries is a nearly intact 40-foot-long "SuperCroc" (Sarcosuchus), the world's largest crocodile. He co-founded Project Exploration, an innovative out-of-school program that exposes city kids to the possibility of scientific careers.*

My parents encouraged all six of their kids to do something interesting with our lives, and we all are college professors. While we were growing up in Naperville, my parents were very progressive. At age eight, I attended a protest march in Chicago led by Martin Luther King, Jr. My mom, an artist, ran safe houses. My dad, a civil engineer/postal worker, had spent time with Dorothy Day's Catholic Worker Movement.★

As a child, I didn't like school because I didn't feel smart. I preferred doing and learning more freely. I have fond memories of many hours spent on my grandfather's 360-acre farm on the outskirts of Naperville. We once took a pig apart from beginning to end and made our own sausage.

I didn't focus on academics until late toward the end of high school when I discovered, finally, that I was talented at something: drawing. That realization was a turning point that provided the impetus for me to apply to Northern Illinois University as an art student. I began noticing things about my drawing. For example, during our life drawing class, I drew the bones within the body rather than the body itself. My interest changed to science quickly and soon focused on paleontology. That shift in direction is an example of why it's so important to remain open to new possibilities, always, as you go through life. Remember, your life plan is not set out before you, and that's part of the fun of it. A good life is one that is unpredictable.

In the early '80s, the most advanced work in paleontology was taking place at Columbia University and the American Museum of Natural History in New York, so that's where I headed. My natural love of hard-core travel and adventure sent me on a trip around the world to write my dissertation in 1984. Traveling alone, I became the first American to return to the Flaming Cliffs, an area of the Gobi Desert that is most famous as the site of the discovery of the first nest of dinosaur eggs and other fossils by American paleontologist Roy Chapman Andrew in the 1920s. Although I don't really believe in luck, within fifteen minutes at the Flaming Cliffs, I discovered my first fossil, a quite famous one with all of the bony elements of the shoulder girdle in place.

When I decided to become a paleontologist, I envisioned it as adventure with a purpose that would be exotic and full of art, travel, history, exploration, and everything fun. On a more practical note, strong leadership skills are required to lead an expedition. My last one, to the Sahara Desert, included twenty students and forty armed guards. I had to know how to fix a car, conduct diplomacy through the U.S. State Department, speak French, and feed and water sixty people – all while accomplishing a scientific objective. The expedition lasted five weeks.

I co-founded a program called Project Exploration in 1999 to make sure that communities traditionally overlooked by science – particularly minority youth and girls – have access to personalized experiences with science and scientists. Our students are more likely to graduate high school, go to college, and major in science than their peers. More than 96 percent of Project Exploration fieldwork participants graduate from high school.

Among other values, my family taught me that I was responsible for making a difference. I look back now to my early school days, and I didn't want to be in the classroom. After-school and out-of-school learning is so important to kids like me, and that's what Project Exploration offers. We are trying to bridge the gap between the ivory tower of education and the genuine act of learning. My advice: Don't miss your chance to make the world a better place.

*Paul Sereno was interviewed on June 6, 2012, at his University of Chicago lab. His birthday is October 11, 1957.*

## Favorites

**BOOK**
*A Sound of Thunder* by Ray Bradbury. A collection of short stories, it features more than thirty of Bradbury's most famous tales, including the arresting title story.

**MOVIE**
*Gladiator* (2000), directed by Ridley Scott. It's a British-American historical drama about love, passion, justice – and winning.

**PERFORMER**
Actor Pierce Brosnan. He's a cool actor and a good friend.

**PLACE**
The hill that slopes gracefully down from the Adler Planetarium.

**SONG**
"Somewhere Over the Rainbow." I like it, especially the version by Israel Kamakawiwo'ole, because it's about dreaming and living a full life.

**QUOTATION**
"Imagination is more important than knowledge."
– ALBERT EINSTEIN, GERMAN-BORN THEORETICAL PHYSICIST

* According to catholicworker.org, "The Catholic Worker Movement is grounded in a firm belief in the God-given dignity of every human person. Today, 227 Catholic Worker communities remain committed to nonviolence, voluntary poverty, prayer and hospitality for the homeless, exiled, hungry, and forsaken. Catholic workers continue to protest injustice, war, racism, and violence of all forms."

"*Imagination is more important...*"

# John Sherer

Organist and Director of Music,
Fourth Presbyterian Church
of Chicago

His spirituality embodies a lifelong quest
to express beauty through music that can
transform the world.

*John W. W. Sherer, Doctor of Musical Arts (DMA), is the Organist and Director of Music at Fourth Presbyterian Church on Chicago's Magnificent Mile. USA Today has selected Fourth Presbyterian Church as one of the top ten places in America to be "enthralled by heavenly music." It is the second-oldest building on Michigan Avenue north of the Chicago River (with the Old Water Tower winning most senior status). Since 1914, more than eight million people have entered under the carved stone tympanum over the Michigan Avenue entrance to the church. The congregation was founded in 1871 and occupied two earlier church buildings before moving to Michigan Avenue.*

*Sherer received two bachelor's degrees in organ performance and music education from the University of Cincinnati College–Conservatory of Music. He then earned two master's degrees at Yale University, one in organ performance and another in art in religion, and received a doctorate in musical arts from the Juilliard School in New York City.*

*Sherer began at Fourth Presbyterian Church in 1996 as full-time organist and director of music. His responsibilities include six choirs, four instrumental ensembles, a dynamic concert series with eighty events a year, and an annual choir tour.*

When I was eleven, a massive tornado hit my hometown of Xenia, Ohio, with absolutely no warning. We ran to our basement to take cover and it was over in an instant. When we returned upstairs we found enormous destruction. The windows of our house had been blown out, walls were embedded with debris, and live electric wires were dancing in the streets. Huge trees had been ripped from the ground and just down the road from us houses were completely gone.

I looked around at this chaos and then sat at the piano and began to play Bach's "Minuet in G Minor." While I wasn't conscious of it at the time, I later realized that for the first time I was using the gift of music to restore beauty and order to a world that desperately needed that gift.

Music called me to be a musician – it found me and never let go. Music is primal to me; it has been with me from the beginning and calls me every day. I have a deep yearning to bring beauty into the world and to allow all people, of all cultures and ages, to share their own gifts of music. I want everyone to experience the transformation that only music and sound can bring to their lives.

I believe notes on sheet music mean nothing until human beings express them. Human beings themselves are like those notes on sheet music. We mean nothing until God expresses Himself through us, until we dwell in God and God sings in and through us. God exists in every human being and, through music, human beings reveal God in each other.

The act of practicing music is very similar to the process of prayer. Both activities require complete attention. Like meditation, music fully absorbs the individual as all extraneous thoughts are shut out. Meditating, or making music, requires the complete emptying of the self and a total focus on the radiant other. All people have gifts to share and can shine more brightly when making music together.

Music binds all of us together over centuries of time. Composers write the music, performers pick up the music, learn the notes, and share them; listeners hear the music for the first time and are eager to hear the familiar melodies again and again. We are all part of an unbroken chain and it is music that binds us together. Someday, I will no longer be able to make music, but I know that the music will live on because someone else will be there to bring beauty to the world.

Even the vibrations of music bind us together in an invisible way. Fourth Presbyterian Church's organ is an Aeolian Skinner, made in 1971. It, like any pipe organ, produces sounds and vibrations that connect each of us to the vibrations of the universe. The sounds are so low and so high that we can barely detect them, and some are so loud that the room literally shakes with the sound. The organ makes you feel larger and lifted up because it is so grand, but it also is humbling because it makes you realize that you are only a small piece of the vast universe.

The source of my spiritual life is an ongoing quest to express beauty through music that will transform the world. In doing so, I connect with the world around me and with everyone who has come before and will come after me. Through music, I pursue beauty in a timeless realm and help others connect to their own spiritual journey.

*John Sherer was interviewed on June 9, 2010, in his office at Fourth Presbyterian Church. His birthday is August 1, 1962.*

## Favorites

**BOOK**
*The Bible.* The poems, letters, and stories from across the centuries provide an endless source of inspiration and an affirmation of God's love.

**MOVIE**
*Titanic* (1997), directed by James Cameron. An epic romantic disaster film, *Titanic* won eleven Academy Awards, including honors for Best Picture and Best Director.

**MUSIC**
Johann Sebastian Bach. "The Passacaglia and Fugue in C Minor" is a stroke of genius that is humbling and inspiring to perform. Many times I've had an out-of-body experience of being pulled upward as I play it. It is as if I am not even the one playing the notes, but that they are emerging from some deep mysterious source.

**PLACE**
Chicago Botanic Garden. I like the sense of being totally connected to and fully engaged with the natural surroundings.

**QUOTATION**
"You are the music while the music lasts."
– T. S. Eliot, American poet, from "The Dry Salvages," one of the poems that comprise *The Four Quartets*.

"You are the music while the music lasts."

# Ed Shurna

## Executive Director, Chicago Coalition for the Homeless

His Lithuanian grandmother's stories of discrimination – encountered in Chicago's infamous stockyards – kindled a determination to fight injustice.

*A quest to answer one absorbing question impels Ed Shurna's journey through life: How do some people overcome, with graciousness and inner strength, the difficulties and even the atrocities that life lobs in their paths? His search for that knowledge plays out in the role of a community organizer (a job title that became familiar to many during the campaign of President Barack Obama) across a range of organizations, those that address education, social justice, gentrification – and especially, homelessness. Shurna grew up in a close and loving home in the working-class Brighton Park neighborhood on Chicago's Southwest Side. He attended Immaculate Conception Church and School and Saint Ignatius High School before spending six years training to become a Jesuit priest at Milford Seminary near Cincinnati, Ohio. Shurna left the order, however, to pursue a life in the outside world – one so hungry for change and in dire need of activism. He holds a B.A. in theology from Loyola University Chicago.*

*Shurna's résumé includes leadership positions at Business Executives for Economic Justice, the Interfaith Organizing Project, and the Harvey Area Community Organization. He apprenticed at the Organization for a Better Austin (1968-1979), where he learned the skills of community organizing under the direction of Tom Gaudette, co-founder of the Mid-America Institute for Community Organizations and a colleague of Saul Alinsky, the dean of Chicago organizers. Shurna joined the Chicago Coalition for the Homeless in 1996, served as director of organizing from 2000-2003, and became executive director in 2003. He has traveled to eight countries to teach, learn, and live with people facing struggles of various sorts.*

Growing up in a neighborhood that was almost totally Lithuanian had a huge influence on me. Brighton Park was a blue-collar community. There was always a sense of people struggling to make a living. My father worked in an office where he serviced the machinery they used. Because my mother had a part-time job, I spent a great amount of time with my grandmother. Like many immigrants, she worked in the Chicago stockyards, the ones that journalist-reformer Upton Sinclair described in his 1906 novel, *The Jungle*. Even as a young boy, when my grandmother told me about the discrimination she'd encountered, I began developing an early sense that the way the world is and the way it *should be* were very different.

Everything in our life revolved around the church, which provided great support and connections through friends and extended family. But life was limited in that everyone I knew was much like me. When I decided to attend Saint Ignatius High School because I wanted to challenge myself, I quickly realized that many of my fellow students experienced very different upbringings. While that situation was difficult to relate to, it also awakened in me many possibilities.

During my last two years in the Jesuits, I trained to become a community organizer. While I very much value pure service work, that which directly helps others, I am more excited by the possibility of creating change. As an organizer, you bring people together to help generate the power for them to change something. When organized in this way, they decide what issues they collectively care about and plan to take action to improve. Organizers don't lead change; that's not our job. These approaches challenge and motivate me. And I find that when you challenge and help support people, they often create positive change.

One of my proudest accomplishments occurred in 1992 when I worked alongside Mabel Manning, a woman who was a mystic, a poet, and a firebrand, at the Interfaith Organizing Project on Chicago's Near West Side. The Chicago Bears wanted to build a stadium in the neighborhood but they wouldn't invest financially in the community. We prevented them from their desired development, but soon after negotiated successfully with the Stadium Joint Venture [Jerry Reinsdorf, owner of the Chicago Bulls, and Bill Wirtz, owner of the Chicago Blackhawks], which resulted in the building of the United Center. The contract resulted in more than 50 million dollars of reinvestment in housing, new parks, a new community library, and more.

When I came to the Chicago Coalition for the Homeless, I'd wrongly presumed that most homeless people were mentally ill; that's just not true. Homelessness is caused by a lack of living-wage jobs and skyrocketing housing costs. Across the U.S., homelessness wasn't a recognized problem until 1980. At that time, Chicago had one shelter; today there are ninety. The answer isn't to build more shelters but rather to solve the problems of poverty that cause homelessness. In a year's time, approximately 102,000 Chicagoans spend some time being homeless. According to Chicago Public Schools, 18,000 of its students spent some period homeless in 2012 – *and 2,500 of them did not even live with an adult but still managed to attend school.*

Every Chicagoan who wants to help the homeless can do so. Donate to organizations that make a difference in solving the problem. Also, I know that many people struggle with whether they should put money in the cup of a homeless person. There's no right or wrong answer to that question. But if a person asks you for money in a decent and cordial way and you choose not to give, don't just ignore them. Rather, acknowledge them with a "No, I'm sorry," or something like that. If a person asks me for money and I have change in my pocket, I usually give it up. It doesn't hurt to give it away.

*Ed Shurna was interviewed on October 24, 2013, at the offices of the Chicago Coalition for the Homeless in the Loop. His birthday is September 25, 1945.*

---

## Favorites

**BOOK**

*Man's Search for Meaning* by Viktor Frankl. According to the *Beacon Press* [beacon.com], "Psychiatrist Viktor Frankl's memoir has riveted generations of readers with its descriptions of life in Nazi death camps and its lessons for spiritual survival. Between 1942 and 1945 Frankl labored in four different camps, including Auschwitz, while his parents, brother, and pregnant wife perished. Based on his own experience and the experiences of others he treated later in his practice, Frankl argues that we cannot avoid suffering but we can choose how to cope with it, find meaning in it, and move forward with renewed purpose."

**MOVIE**

*The Godfather* (1972), directed by Francis Ford Coppola and based on the novel by Mario Puzo. It's an epic fight between good and evil.

**POET**

Gerard Manley Hopkins, a Jesuit poet. His use of language is colorful and expressive.

**QUOTATION**

"Find God in all things."

— A TENET OF JESUIT SPIRITUALITY

*Find God in all things.*

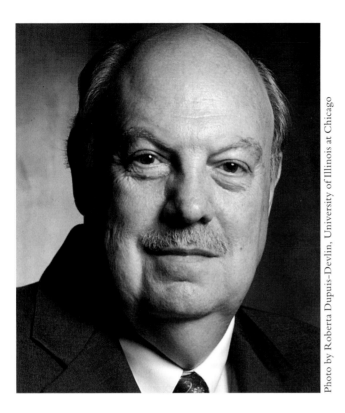

# Dick Simpson

## Political Reformer and Professor

Using experiences shaped by the civil rights movement, he courageously confronted Chicago's political machine.★

*"Indefatigable" is one of the many adjectives you might ascribe to Dick Simpson, Ph.D., M.Div., Chairman, Department of Political Science, University of Illinois at Chicago. He is the stuff of living legend in local political circles. Simpson enjoys a distinguished academic career of more than forty-five years that is hallmarked by public service in city government and political activism. During the turbulent political tides that rocked Chicago, specifically, from 1975-1989, he was the two-term alderman of the 44th Ward and leader of the opposition bloc in the Chicago City Council. In that role – one he bucked the system to win –Simpson spearheaded the opposition against mayors Richard J. Daley and Michael Bilandic. Among his twenty book titles is* Rogues, Rebels and Rubber Stamps: The Politics of the Chicago City Council from 1863 to the Present.

*Simpson joined the faculty of the University of Illinois at Chicago in 1967 and was named Chair of the Department of Political Science in 2006. His academic specialties embrace Chicago politics, elections, state and local politics, neighborhood empowerment, and public corruption. Born in Houston, Texas, Dr. Simpson earned his doctorate at Indiana University. An ordained minister of the United Church of Christ, he served at Chicago's Wellington Avenue Church from 1985-2005.*

Although nobody in my immediate family was a political leader, university professor, or minister, there was a history – on both sides – of teaching and preaching. My interest in politics stemmed from early leadership in the Boy Scouts of America. I earned the equivalent of three Eagle Scout awards [the highest rank attainable] and through the Order of the Arrow, the national honor society of the Boy Scouts, assumed leadership roles within the Houston metropolitan region. My first teaching opportunity was as a Boy Scout camp counselor.

I became political in college, first at Texas A&M and then at the University of Texas. One of my life's turning points was my involvement during the civil rights movement. When I was twenty-one, 200 of us were trying to integrate theaters and restaurants. People threw bottles at us. Our first meeting was bombed. Through those experiences, I learned about the techniques that those in power practice to keep protesters quiet. For example, they won't turn on your microphone, and they will try to force you to sit. There is a famous photo of me in the Chicago City Council chambers in 1971 in which the sergeant-at-arms and a policeman are trying to make me sit, even though, as an alderman, I had every right to stand and be heard.

I consider myself an idealist with a great deal of pragmatic experience about how to translate ideals into reality. You must be an idealist with a very strong set of beliefs in order to pursue the kind of path that I've taken.

I moved to Chicago in 1967 to begin my career at the University of Illinois at Chicago. About that time, I became part of the Alternative Convention Campaign, which operated almost as a third-party movement to elect Eugene McCarthy. I then supported the McCarthy for President Campaign in the Democratic Party. When I criticized the action of the campaign, they appointed me an organizer of the 9th congressional district in Chicago and, later, campaign manager for Illinois.

Why did politics appeal to me? Because I wanted to fix all the problems of the world. To do that, you have to win elections and control government. It is a craft, and I learned how to do it. My book, *Winning Elections: A Handbook of Participatory Politics,* remains in print after forty years.

When I became an alderman in 1971, my objective was to increase citizen participation in local government. I created a ward assembly, with wide representation from local community groups. As long as they agreed by a two-thirds majority, their decisions determined my vote in the city council. This approach was unique in Chicago. Later, when I led the opposition bloc against mayors Daley and Bilandic, I had the strong support of many voters on the North Side who also believed machine politics was bad for Chicago. It was frightening at times; when I ran for alderman, I received death threats.

Later in life, as an ordained minister, I developed the spiritual aspect of my life that had been virtually dormant during my politically active years. Different periods of one's life call for different emphases. I've come to envision goals that aren't strictly political and to value meditation in the Christian tradition, especially related to prayer and techniques such as journaling.

*Dick Simpson was interviewed on January 13, 2012, at his academic office at the University of Illinois at Chicago. His birthday is November 8, 1940.*

## Favorites

### BOOKS ON POLITICS
*Rules for Radicals* by Saul Alinsky: In organizing, I've been most influenced by this book because it tells how to organize communities of people without power and tells them how to get power; *Boss* by Mike Royko: I assign this book, about former Mayor Richard J. Daley, every semester in the class I teach about Chicago politics; and *Don't Make No Waves, Don't Back No Losers: An Insider's Analysis of the Daley Machine* by Milton Rakove.

### PLAY
*Henry V* by William Shakespeare. I enjoy his historical dramas, especially this one.

### POETS
Irish poet W. B. Yeats. I like him for his mysticism and his political nature. Another poet I admire is my friend Chicago poet Mark Perlberg, who died recently.

### QUOTATION
"If it is not worth doing, it is not worth doing well."
— RICHARD JOHNSON, MY PREDECESSOR AS CHAIR OF THE POLITICAL SCIENCE DEPARTMENT

* According to the *Encyclopedia Britannica,* a political machine, in U.S. politics, is a party organization, headed by a single boss or small autocratic group, which commands enough votes to maintain political and administrative control of a city, county, or state.

"*If it is not worth doing...*"

# Alpana Singh

## Master Sommelier

Her palate, tenacity, and culinary acumen uncork a talent of rare vintage.

*More than a decade ago at this writing, at age twenty-six, Alpana Singh became the youngest woman to join the ranks of the Court of Master Sommeliers,★ the elite body that administers the intensive, days-long exam that aspiring sommeliers must pass to earn the coveted Master Sommelier credential. Four years earlier, Alpana Singh displayed her trademark self-confidence when she relocated from her family's California home to Chicago after unexpectedly landing the plum position of sommelier at Chicago's Everest Restaurant, located on the 40th floor of the Chicago Stock Exchange.*

*Her book,* Alpana Pours: About Being a Woman, Loving Wine & Having Great Relationships, *welcomes readers into the flavorful world of wine by making the subject what she reminds us it should be – fun! Formerly, she was the Director of Wine and Spirits for Lettuce Entertain You Enterprises and host of the Emmy Award-winning TV program "Check, Please!" In 2012, with partners, she opened The Boarding House, a Chicago fine-dining establishment.*

Until 1975, my parents lived in Fiji, as did many Indian emigrants. They moved to Monterey, California – where a large contingent of Fijian Indians also resided – a year before my birth. As the first members of both of their families to resettle in a new country, there was a strong obligation to foster other newcomers. In that role, my mother became an outgoing pillar of the community. During the twenty-three years I lived at home, some twenty different people lived with us. While our life was sociable and boisterous, it also was tumultuous. You had to speak loudly to be heard. I liked the feeling of belonging to an extended community, but the challenge was that young people are considered a strong reflection of their parents in Indian families. When I moved to Chicago at twenty-three, I was eager to begin an independent life.

As a teenager, I often was stubborn and defiant, never taking "no" for an answer. Like many Indian parents, my parents expected me to go to college. At eighteen, I needed money for my education and applied at a fine-dining restaurant in Monterey, Montrio Bistro. I was not hired initially because I knew nothing about wine. I really needed the job so I spent the entire next weekend reading *Wine for Dummies* and, as a result, was then offered the position immediately. That's how I problem solve – decide what I need to accomplish, step by step, and complete the next task that will help accomplish my goal. Rather than accept "no," I drill down and – when necessary – figure out if I can change someone's mind.

As it turned out, college bored me out of my mind but I became increasingly fascinated with wine. I experienced an awakening: Maybe I could become a sommelier. The manager at Montrio encouraged me and recommended I seek a job at a wine shop. [Note: She even offered to work for free.] Essentially, the decision had been made. And once I decide something, *it's done.* Considerable contention arose when I told my mother I was quitting college and instead would work in a wine shop while continuing as a restaurant server. In Hinduism, the deity Brahma is devoted to education and higher learning. Education and religion are completely intertwined. In my mother's mind, I worked at a liquor store and served drinks; in my mind I was training to become a sommelier.

Jean Joho, chef/proprietor of Chicago's Everest restaurant, one of the country's premier dining rooms, took a chance by hiring me as his sommelier at the young age of twenty-three. I was a wild stallion of unbridled energy in need of mentoring, shaping, toning. My dress and accessories – including colorful plastic jewelry and service etiquette – were sometimes inappropriate. He taught me how to present myself. Luck intervened, too. I happened to meet Chef Joho, coincidentally, only minutes after Claudine Pépin of PBS shared a glowing endorsement of me with a mutual friend because I'd passed the advanced sommelier examination at age twenty-one. That individual then shared the story with Chef Joho, who offered me a job that very day.

Talented sommeliers must be passionate about history, sociology, travel, culture, art, food, and science. We are individuals with diverse interests that just happen to culminate in a neat little package called wine.

*Alpana Singh was interviewed at a coffee shop in the Streeterville neighborhood on May 23, 2012. Her birthday is November 29, 1976.*

---

## Favorites

**BOOK**
*One Hundred Years of Solitude* by Gabriel García Márquez. The final twenty pages of the book were the reward for the three years it took me to read it.

**NONPROFIT**
Trio Animal Foundation, Chicago. The organization assists shelters, rescues, and individuals by paying the medical bills of homeless pets. I grew up with a menagerie of dogs, cats, chickens – and even a duck.

**PERFORMER**
Madonna. I love how she continues reinventing herself.

**QUOTATION**
"Everyone brings wine. I bring bread."
— LARRY DAVID, AMERICAN ACTOR, WRITER, COMEDIAN, AND TELEVISION PRODUCER

---

* Sommeliers are responsible for wine and beverage selection at an establishment, including maintenance of the list, service, and the training required to help create environments in which guests can savor complementary food and wine pairings. The Court of Master Sommeliers was established to encourage and improve the standards of beverage knowledge and service in hotels and restaurants. As of February 2014, 135 professionals had earned the title of Master Sommelier in North America. Of that number, 116 were men and nineteen were women. There are 214 professional sommeliers worldwide who have received the title of Master Sommelier since the first Master Sommelier Diploma Exam.

*"Everyone brings wine. I bring bread."*

# Gary Slutkin

## Founder and Executive Director, Cure Violence

He developed, and now applies internationally, a powerful public health approach to stopping our country's epidemic of gun violence.

*Epidemiologist Gary Slutkin, M.D., is founder and executive director of Cure Violence (formerly CeaseFire), a scientifically proven approach to violence reduction. In creating Cure Violence, Slutkin applied lessons learned from more than a decade with the World Health Organization and in helping people battle tuberculosis in San Francisco, cholera in Mogadishu, and AIDS in Uganda. He received his M.D. from the University of Chicago Pritzker School of Medicine and completed his internship and residency at San Francisco General Hospital. Closer to home, the native Chicagoan is radically redefining traditional approaches to reducing gun (and other forms of) violence. Cure Violence's influence, both on the domestic and international fronts, took shape on Chicago's South and West Sides. Today, Cure Violence operates in 15 U.S. cities and several countries.*

Growing up on the North Side of Chicago, *science* was my religion. My parents were Jewish by birth but did not practice or even talk about that aspect of their past. Judaism had a difficult history that they did not like to discuss. My father was a research chemist. As a child, I visited his lab. While I didn't understand what his work consisted of, and it seemed mysterious, I also thought, "There are answers there." Any form of social injustice unsettled my mother, and she was the greatest influence on me. From my parents' conversations about what was happening in the news, I formed ideas about what was fair, and unfair, in the world.

I'm driven to learn, explore, and understand things. That's why I went to medical school and why I chose the field of infectious disease. I am aware of wanting to do as much as I possibly can. I just see specific work that clearly needs to be done, and I take on those assignments. I'm motivated to do as much as I can while I'm here. Otherwise, why am I here?

When I returned to Chicago in 1995 after working on epidemics in Asia and Africa, I couldn't imagine identifying a large-scale public health issue to take on, compared with what I'd seen in other parts of the world. Friends suggested I look at the violence epidemic. I began by designing a strategy – as we did at the World Health Organization – to explore how behaviors are formed, maintained, and changed.

When I talk to groups about Cure Violence, many people act as if it's a new idea to look at reducing violence from a scientific perspective. It's difficult to imagine that in the twenty-first century, we would view an issue like violence moralistically when we can apply effective, concrete approaches that are grounded in scientific method. Yes, violence has been around since the history of mankind, but many infectious diseases are now part of the past.

The idea is to make the use of violence socially unacceptable, much like smoking in public places has now become. The methods we use involve changing people's thinking, social change, incorporating cognitive psychology, and brain research. Our method is to help those at greatest risk of violent behavior be more aware of their thoughts and emotions – and then develop a less reactive relationship to them.

Many strategies are employed, including the use of outreach workers, often former gang members, as "violence interrupters."★★ They defuse group rivalries, identify potential altercations, and prevent retaliation for violence that's already occurred. Usually – especially without an intervention – one act of violence predicts the next act of violence. [Note: A study of Cure Violence's outreach in Chicago by the U.S. Department of Justice documented reductions in shootings and killings, ranging from 41 percent to 73 percent, in the neighborhoods in which Cure Violence operated.]

When I consider the concept of spirituality, I include a view of the invisible. Before the microscope was invented, we didn't realize there were invisible microorganisms. There's a lot of stuff going on that we don't see. There's another level other than what we see, and it keeps everything going and interconnected. We all emerge out of that place, as do our thoughts. Reducing violence involves changing those invisible thoughts.

*Gary Slutkin was interviewed on November 3, 2010, at the offices of Cure Violence, located at the University of Illinois at Chicago. His birthday is July 8, 1950.*

---

## Favorites

**ACTOR**
Jack Nicholson. He's such an individual, and he says exactly what he wants to say.

**MOVIE**
*Team America: World Police* (2004), directed by Trey Parker (of *South Park* fame). It's a hilarious satire on terrorism and heroic antiterrorism as enacted by puppets.

**MUSIC**
"A Love Supreme" by jazz saxophone player John Coltrane. I find this music to be so powerful that I've only listened to it a half-dozen times.

**POET**
Rumi, the thirteenth-century Persian Sufi mystic. He's airy, and he takes you somewhere.

**QUOTATION**
"Do you remember how electrical currents and 'unseen waves' were laughed at? The knowledge about man is still in its infancy."
— ALBERT EINSTEIN, GERMAN-BORN THEORETICAL PHYSICIST

---

★ The Illinois program of Cure Violence still operates under its original name, CeaseFire.

★★ A documentary based on the work of Cure Violence, "The Interrupters," premiered at Sundance in 2011 and later aired on PBS's FRONTLINE.

"*The knowledge about man...*"

# Mary Sommers

## "The Mother of All Midwives"

She helps new mothers embrace the primal strength that, she believes, resonates instinctively and deeply from their very cores.

*Witness to nearly 1,500 births over three decades, Mary Sommers, CPM (Certified Professional Midwife), MPS (Masters in Public Service), is a leader, mentor, and maternal figure in Chicago's midwife community. She is the site director of the Erie Family Health Center's Humboldt Park location and Director of Academic Affairs of the Midwest Maternal Child Institute in Oregon, Wisconsin. As a World Health Organization fellow in 1994, she focused her studies on maternal health and breastfeeding programs in Holland and England. Sommers has supervised more than forty midwifery students and trained more than fifty doulas.★ She earned a bachelor's in women's studies from Northeastern Illinois University and holds a master's in public service with an emphasis on international public service from DePaul University in Chicago.*

*By the writing of text books/guide books and serving in not-for-profit educational roles, Sommers is also engaged with midwifery education in Mexico and Malawi. She works on video and other educational projects, brings U.S. students with her to gain clinical experience, and continues to work as a midwife in these countries.*

*In her book* More than a Midwife, *published in 2011, Sommers shares stories of the glory, grace, and joy – as well as the heartbreak and tragedy – that she's experienced through her twenty-plus years of working with mothers and their infants.*

As one of thirteen children growing up in Detroit, I knew a radical nun who was a missionary in Ghana, as well as a midwife. That turned out to be a good thing; when I decided I wanted to become a midwife, my parents didn't think it was a completely crackpot thing to do. Sister Anne demonstrated a commitment of service that was very appealing. Social justice is an important aspect of my life, and midwifery seemed like one way to follow that path. I think of midwifery as one part science, one part feminism, and one part spiritual calling.

I was raised in a traditional Catholic family. Like many big Catholic families of the '60s and '70s, mine was socially progressive. Today, my beliefs lie in the realm of Christian mysticism. [Note: Bernard McGinn, professor emeritus at the University of Chicago Divinity School, defines Christian mysticism as a form of spirituality that "concerns the preparation for, the consciousness of, and the reaction to . . . the immediate or direct presence of God."] The mystics – people like twelfth-century German abbess Hildegard of Bingen, twelfth-century Saint Clare of Assisi, and fourteenth-century English philosopher Julian of Norwich [a woman] – have spoken to me in a way that has resonated since I was a young girl. We don't feel God by reading about God, but rather by being aware of God's presence as a "felt "experience.

The mystics convey a sense of play, awe, and wonder. When a seed is planted and a flower grows, we explain that occurrence scientifically, but isn't that process – and its power – also a sign of God's presence and mystery? And look at childbirth: The mother/baby dyad often instinctively knows what to do when left to its own devices. We've lost some of our instinctual knowledge as we've become more intellectual about natural processes. As a result, we need to balance science and art with instinct. The classes I teach let women reclaim that inner knowledge that comes from instinct and from the deep places in us that are primal and spiritual.

Every time I witness a birth, I am aware of my soul; birth is a mystical experience. Obviously, labor is a long and hard process for most first-time mothers. And unfortunately, many women have let society convince them that they can't do the "hard thing" that is birth. Even professional women who graduated from law school, climbed Mount Kilimanjaro, or completed marathons sometimes confide that they don't think they'll be able to endure a natural childbirth process. However, we only do the difficult things in life because they're anchored to our deeper values and our deeper sense of ourselves. And when we do these hard things, that experience becomes an important element of who we are; that's why birth is transformative. I don't advocate one kind of birth for everyone and I'm not against epidurals or other interventions across the board, but I do feel strongly that women should be conscious about their choices.

At this point in my life, I am more interested in how we train midwives than I am in anything else. Education and international work will be a large part of my future focus. I'm drawn to the idea that we're all part of one big planet.

*Mary Sommers was interviewed at the offices of Comprehensive Wellness Care in Lincoln Park on February 18, 2011. Her birthday is September 10, 1960.*

## Favorites

**BOOK**
*What Is the What* by Dave Eggers. In this exceptional novel, the history of Sudan's civil war is recounted through the eyes of Valentino Achak Deng, a refugee who immigrates to the U.S.

**MOVIE**
*Black Robe* (1991), directed by Bruce Beresford. Set in the seventeenth century, the movie's story revolves around a Jesuit priest and a young companion who are guided through the Quebec wilderness by Algonquin Indians to find a distant mission in the dead of winter.

**MUSIC**
"The Green Fields of France," an Irish ballad, and "Be Not Too Hard," written by Joan Baez and performed by Donovan. I want these songs to be played at my funeral because they illustrate the importance of compassion and shared humanity. We're not always our best selves – but sometimes we are.

**PLACE**
The woods. I love to walk there when it's misty, damp, and swampy beneath my feet; that feels like home to me.

**QUOTATION**
"To know and not to act is not to know."
– ATTRIBUTED TO LAO-TSE, THE FIRST PHILOSOPHER OF THE TAOIST SCHOOL

* Doulas are experienced professionals who provide continuous physical, emotional and informational support to mothers before, during and just after birth..

"*To know and not to act is not to know.*"

# David Steinhorn

## Pediatric Palliative Care Physician

Lifelong student of the spirituality of living, death, and dying urges individuals to pay greater attention to lessons each of us is called upon to experience.

*David Steinhorn, M.D, was the medical director of The Bridges Program for Pediatric Palliative Care at Lurie Children's Hospital (formerly Children's Memorial Hospital) in Chicago from 2005-2011. In 2013, he joined the faculty of the University of California-Davis Children's Hospital in Sacramento, California, as a pediatric critical care and palliative care physician. (Palliative care strives to give meaning and quality to life through the management of pain, symptoms, and the stress of serious illness. It is not the same thing as hospice care at the very end of life – although hospice always includes palliative care.)*

*In 2003, Steinhorn co-founded the Judith Nan Joy Integrative Medicine Initiative, which sought to create a new model for hospital-based pediatric healthcare by integrating conventional allopathic protocols with complementary therapies, such as touch healing, massage, and acupuncture. He graduated from the University of Minnesota Medical School. Steinhorn says that above all else, his professional and personal passion is to bring light and awareness of the human spirit into institutional pediatric healthcare and into his own life.*

I grew up in a Jewish household in the Rogers Park neighborhood of Chicago and was bar mitzvahed; however, Jewish services never resonated with me. My father, who'd grown up in an Orthodox Jewish household, experienced a great deal of ambivalence connected to his upbringing. He never found a constructive way to deal with his pain, and he committed suicide on my eighteenth birthday. That act of desperation catapulted me into seeking a beneficial way to deal with the loss, and I've been on a spiritual quest ever since.

I experienced an epiphany after reading *Many Lives, Many Masters: The True Story of a Prominent Psychiatrist, His Young Patient, and the Past-Life Therapy That Changed Both Their Lives,* by Brian Weiss, M.D. Reading about his experiences with patients who talked in detail about their past lives convinced me that this stuff is probably real.

A challenging aspect of medicine for the majority of physicians in the West is the separation between the physical nature of illness and the emotional and spiritual implications of being ill. The Western approach neglects the multidimensional nature of the human spirit. Historically, physicians didn't possess all the drugs and the technology that we have now, but they were often more available psychologically and emotionally.

Any deep level of illness carries with it a profound opportunity to learn, a wake-up call to discover what, exactly, life is asking us to experience. Our lives are mirrors reflecting back to us that which needs to be examined. The question is not simply, "What does the body require to be cured?" but also, "What do the soul and the spirit need in order to be healed?" Contemporary Western medicine doesn't have a clue, but many traditional healing methods – including Reiki, a Japanese energy healing technique for stress reduction and relaxation that also promotes healing; Qigong, a Chinese system of working with chi, or life energy; and Shamanism, the spiritual practices of ancient civilizations and cultures – help individuals to be more open to life's lessons.

The palliative care movement began in the late 1960s. Because there was no accepted alternative to further therapy, patients were offered additional medical treatments, even though their potential for living a good-quality life – or any life at all – was nil. There was, finally, recognition that there is not always another treatment to offer.

Pediatrics led the way in advancing palliative care by introducing the concept of referral to palliative care earlier in the treatment process. Traditionally, palliative and hospice care had only been considered during the last seven to fourteen days of life, when a patient was literally at the brink of death. However, that's too brief a time to develop a rapport with families, understand their values, and work most effectively to discover the remaining lessons of life.

Hospice care evolved as a counter-culture movement: Many patients were abandoned by the traditional care system when there were no further therapies or surgery to offer. Patients didn't want to be cared for by, say, an oncologist, who would primarily treat their cancer and its symptoms, only to be sent away when the oncologist had nothing further to offer. Instead, they preferred the idea of a team of individuals, as in hospice, that tends to their physical needs as well as their spiritual needs. This group includes physicians, nurses, social workers, chaplains, music therapists, Healing Touch★ therapists, and others. Especially when they are dying, people deserve to be treated with dignity and compassion as intrinsically valuable human beings, for whatever time may remain. The care providers also gain much through the sacred work of attending to a dying person.

*Dr. Steinhorn was interviewed at Children's Memorial Hospital in Lincoln Park on November 15, 2010. (The new Lurie Children's Hospital is located in Streeterville.) His birthday is May 30, 1950.*

<table>
<tr><td colspan="2" style="text-align:center">— Favorites —</td></tr>
<tr><td colspan="2">

**BOOK**
*Faust,* the play by German writer Johann Wolfgang von Goethe. It is the story of a man who constantly strove to understand the inner workings of creation and his place in it. He was tormented and unable to find peace because he could not say to any experience, "Verweile doch, du bist so schön." (In English, "Stay a while, you are so beautiful.")

**MOVIE**
*Zardoz* (1974), directed by John Boorman. Starring Sean Connery, this is a quirky dystopian science fiction/fantasy.

**MUSIC**
Gustav Mahler's Fifth and Ninth Symphonies and Beethoven's Seventh Symphony.

**POET**
Johann Wolfgang von Goethe.

**QUOTATION**
"There are more things in heaven and earth, Horatio, than are dreamt of in your philosophy."
— WILLIAM SHAKESPEARE, BRITISH PLAYWRIGHT AND POET, FROM *HAMLET*

</td></tr>
</table>

★ Healing Touch is a relaxing, nurturing energy therapy through which gentle touch assists in balancing one's physical, mental, emotional, and spiritual well-being. The practice works with an individual's energy field to support its natural ability to heal.

"*more things in heaven and earth...*"

# Tony Tasset
## Conceptual Artist

His sense of humor, interactive approach, and populist bent connect him to "Joe Six-Pack."

*With tongue firmly planted in cheek at times, conceptual artist Tony Tasset's motto might well be "Go big or go home." First trained as a painter, his prolific output now includes video, photography, bronze, wax, film, and even taxidermy. But Chicagoans know him best as the creator of the fiberglass sculpture "Eye," a 30-foot high spherical eyeball that millions of locals and tourists couldn't resist making eye contact with when it dominated the Loop's Pritzker Park in the summer of 2010. Commissioned by the Chicago Loop Alliance, "Eye" was chosen for the high-exposure display because it impressed the selection committee with playfulness, irreverence, and "Everyman" appeal.*

*Tasset's work is displayed internationally in galleries and museums. Over the past decade, his inventive designs – or public art – have attracted increasing interest from both cities and corporations. Next up is a nine-story steel rainbow sculpture for Sony Pictures Entertainment's Culver City, California, studio. Born in Cincinnati, Ohio, Tasset received his bachelor of fine arts at the Art Academy of Cincinnati and his master's of fine arts at Chicago's School of the Art Institute. The Oak Park resident is a professor of art at the University of Illinois at Chicago.*

One of my early memories is of my mom giving me paper so I could draw while we sat in a pew at church. A dabbler herself, she particularly encouraged the idea of my becoming an artist. Like many parents, my mother and father possessed an almost pathological belief in their children's abilities to succeed. Also, the nuns in my grade school drilled into students the idea that each of us had a talent that could be developed, and I always envisioned my future as an artist.

I signed up for a correspondence course in art and began taking drawing classes in grammar school. I wasn't interested in fine art. My early influences were Walt Disney, Norman Rockwell, and *Mad* magazine before moving on to minimalism and conceptual art.

I consider myself fortunate to be a professor at the University of Illinois at Chicago, a research institution, as well as a working artist. I like teaching because it represents art without the hype – art that hasn't gone through the wringer of the system. The work hasn't been prejudged, so I can respond on my own with no preconceived thoughts. My students often ask me how to get their work placed in galleries, and I tell them to create art that can't be ignored. I also tell them that being an artist is a *job*, not only a passion. I've been working nonstop since graduate school.

There's a lot of intimidation surrounding the idea of becoming an artist. I was lucky in that I never considered another career – this was it for me. I am appreciative of the success I've achieved, but the reason I'm successful is that I never *feel* successful. The biggest challenge I face is self-doubt, and I don't know if I have overcome it. I go all out with every piece I make.

"Eye" received a good deal of acclaim, but let's face it, a 30-foot eyeball can't go unnoticed. I love the Calder "Flamingo" and the Picasso sculpture in Daley Plaza, but I was after something kitschier and more populist, a piece that could appeal to Joe Six-Pack. Everyone who saw "Eye" got it on some level. A work like "Eye" absorbs a lot of meanings; the eye historically is a symbol of god, power, consciousness, and what it means to be human.

I'm not interested in decorating a space with my art. I want to make art that interacts with people and is a force to be reckoned with. When I'm making public art, I think of myself as a communicator. Creating public art is not like making art for the "white box" of a gallery. Instead, you're competing with the city itself for attention.

Working in a very large scale is one way of grabbing that focus. "Eye" operates as both art and spectacle. Many people loved it, but some didn't. That's okay, because I've always wanted to make art that people either love or hate.

*Tony Tasset was interviewed at a Chicago residence on December 15, 2012. His birthday is October 16, 1960.*

---

## Favorites

**ARTIST**
Andy Warhol. He is a primary influence because of the scale of his vision. Much of what he prophesized has come true – like the idea that everybody will be famous for fifteen minutes.

**BOOK**
*Let's Talk About Love: A Journey to the End of Taste* by Carl Wilson. It's a discourse on how individuals define themselves within the confines of what they perceive as good or bad, hip or square.

**MOVIE**
*Blue Velvet* (1986), directed by David Lynch. It was "our movie" in the 1980s.

**PERFORMERS**
Bob Dylan and Neil Young. Maybe it's because I'm getting older, but their music means a lot to me now. Dylan is more the artist – sarcastic and cryptic – but Neil Young inspires me by wearing his heart on his sleeve.

**QUOTATION**
"I can't help it if I'm lucky."
— BOB DYLAN, AMERICAN MUSICIAN, A LYRIC FROM "IDIOT WIND"

"*I can't help it if I'm lucky.*"

# Bronwyn Weaver

## (Queen) Beekeeper

Honeybees sweeten her days with relaxation, immersion in nature, and a sense of wonder.

*Bronwyn Weaver is a co-owner of Heritage Prairie Farm, an organic farm and market in rural LaFox, located in Kane County. A riotous mélange of vegetables, fruits, and herbs thrive on the thirteen-acre plot, but it's the 150 beehives nurtured here that stake the strongest claim on Weaver's heart. Her awe at the complexity of apiary culture is reinforced by an intense knowledge of the life-sustaining role the creatures play in all things agricultural. (A recent four-year study by Cornell University found that bee pollination enhances U.S. crop value by almost $15 billion per year.) She holds a B.S. in Geology from Ohio's Case Western University.*

Growing up in Akron, Ohio, the youngest of four daughters, our family lived a comfortable life. My father was in the plastics business, and my mother was active in the country club. All that changed at age four when one my sisters died after being struck by lightning. It happened in 1968, back when people didn't talk much about their feelings after experiencing this kind of a tragedy. Rather, we just got through it.

A few years later, when my parents emerged from their haze of grief, Dad had an epiphany: After flushing all the pain-numbing barbiturates – which were prescribed to everyone in the family except me – down the toilet, he sold his business interests and decided to buy an organic farm. At age fifty-two, when I was seven, my parents launched a new life for us on a 160-acre farm just south of Akron. It was a radical choice, and one that healed our family.

I loved life on the farm, but I never thought about what I specifically liked or didn't like about our life. It was just what we did. The farm was never intended as a commercial enterprise. My Dad was immensely likable with a joyous personality, and he continued his successful involvement with business projects. He provided the energy while my mother, whose family had deep agrarian roots, was the peaceful influence and the scholar. My parents are my greatest influences, my yin and my yang.

Our move to the farm ultimately propelled my entire life. I experienced a joyous upbringing that stemmed from plugging into the satisfaction that comes from hard work. It *is* exhausting. I usually work six and a half days a week; it's virtually a necessity because of today's pressured business climate.

At seven, I began working with the hives and never felt any fear. I learned early on how important bees are. Every farming endeavor begins with bees because they are so critical to pollination and the setting of seeds. The taste of fruits and vegetables, whether they're delicious or not, depends on the quality of their pollination.

There's no better lesson about sustainability in farming than the role of bees. For example, if the dairy industry lost 60 percent of its herd every year, can you imagine the ramifications and the uproar that would result? That's exactly what's happening to beekeeping. [Note: Weaver is referring to the well-documented phenomenon of Colony Collapse Disorder, which occurs when worker bees from a beehive or colony abruptly disappear. The term *Colony Collapse Disorder* was first applied to a drastic rise in the number of disappearances of Western honeybee colonies in 2006.] In response to the crisis, many modern beekeepers are adapting our methods to enhance sustainability.

Being a beekeeper enriches my life. The process requires an approach that is calm, slow, and steady. The bees – *not you* – dictate the pace at which you will work. Because they're temperamental, bees are sensitive to your ability to work with them. On good days, I can go out to my bees without wearing a veil or gloves, open the hives, and just talk to the bees. It's the most peaceful and realigning experience you can imagine. For me, beekeeping is a meditation.

I was raised in the Episcopalian Church, and I still attend services. A line from the 1928 *Book of Common Prayer* that always resonates with me is that we will be fed by God's holy mysteries. That is my approach to beekeeping, which is essential to my spiritual life.

There are some aspects of beekeeping that we simply can't explain, and I'm fine with that. For example, beeswax and royal jelly can't be chemically duplicated. These mysterious gifts from nature nurture my faith. Beekeeping, and all the beautiful things that come from the hive, enable me to be fed and rejuvenated.

*Bronwyn Weaver was interviewed at Heritage Prairie Farm on September 10, 2011. Her birthday is December 18, 1964.*

## Favorites

**BOOK FOR ASPIRING BEEKEEPERS**
*The Backyard Beekeeper: An Absolute Beginner's Guide to Keeping Bees in Your Yard and Garden* by Kim Flottum.

**MOVIE**
*Enchanted April* (1991), directed by Mike Newell. It's based on Elizabeth von Arnim's 1922 novel, *The Enchanted April.*

**NONPROFIT**
Heifer International. It's an organization that works with communities to end hunger and poverty and care for the earth by empowering lives with self-reliance and hope, primarily through gifts of livestock.

**PLACE**
I live in the middle of a sacred space. As a result, I pray continually; that's a change from a decade ago.

**QUOTATION**
"The beginning of wisdom is to call things by their right names."
— CHINESE PROVERB

*"The beginning of wisdom..."*

Photo by Stephen Green Photography

# Kerry Wood

## Philanthropist and Former Chicago Cub

Wunderkind who played on his own terms ranks among Wrigley Field's treasured alums.

*Born into a close-knit, sports-loving family, Kerry Wood debuted on the baseball diamond in Irving, Texas, at age five and unleashed his pitching passion by fourteen. At age fifteen, when thirty-five scouts showed up to check out a player on an opposing team, they were wowed by Wood's prowess – placing him on the radar before he was old enough to drive.*

*Wood joined the minor leagues at age seventeen and began the first of two stretches as a Chicago Cub at twenty. In only his fifth career start with the Cubs, "Kid K" pitched a game that is considered one of the most impressive performances in baseball history – a one-hit, no-walk, twenty-strikeout shutout against the Houston Astros. Months later, he was named Major League Rookie of the Year. Although his fourteen-year run was beset with injuries that caused Kerry Wood to retire sooner than he'd have liked, the two-time National League All-Star expresses immense pride in his baseball career, one that yielded home runs for humanity, generosity, and team leadership. He remains with the Cubs organization in a mentoring role as special assistant to the president of the Chicago Cubs.*

*Even before he retired in 2012, Wood and his wife, Sarah, began channeling the benefits of his high-profile persona into philanthropy. Since 2011, they've raised more than $3 million for charities that serve children through their Wood Family Foundation, whose mission focuses on improving the lives of children and youth in the Chicago area through raising funds for a variety of programs. One new initiative offers full-ride scholarships to the University of Illinois at Chicago for selected high-achievers from the underserved neighborhoods on which the foundation concentrates – Englewood, Austin, Lawndale, and Humboldt Park.*

*Wood is especially proud of Sarah's commitment to their cause. "She's passionate about it and volunteers many, many hours of her time," he explains. The foundation was designed as a family affair and as a possible family legacy. "It's important for us to model generosity for our kids. Last year, they raised money for the foundation by setting up a lemonade stand." Kerry Wood was named "Father of the Year" in 2011 by the Illinois Fatherhood Initiative. "The trophy stays on the mantel so my wife can see it every morning," he jokes.*

When my brother and I were little, our dad promised us that he would always play sports with us if we asked. When we wanted to join teams, he told us we'd have to attend every practice and not miss any games. We learned about commitment – that others rely on you to be part of the team – at a young age. That lesson stays with me as the father of three young children: Justin, Katie, and Charlotte.

My first taste of adversity came when I was eighteen. During my second semi-pro season, with the Daytona Cubs, I started pitching terribly. I couldn't improve the situation no matter how I tried, so I was preparing to give up and go home. While I was packing my bags, the farm director paid me a visit. He acknowledged my frustration and sat me down to reassure me things would get better. He reminded me that the team had made a huge commitment to me, and I needed to honor it. That really sunk in. I returned the next day with a better attitude and ready to work.

When I arrived in Chicago to join the major leagues, I was absolutely terrified. At twenty, I'd never even been in a taxi. The only place I was comfortable was on the field. I certainly didn't feel great in the clubhouse, with media people and cameras everywhere. I learned a lot from watching veteran players like Kevin Tapani, my locker mate during my rookie season. I admired how he handled the media, talked easily about his family, and hung his kids' artwork in his locker.

The best memory of my career wasn't the twenty-strikeout shutout; rather, it was the day I played my last game in 2012. In 2007, I had an inoperable rotator cuff injury. At the time, my son, Justin, was only six months old. Even though everyone told me I'd never pitch again, I was highly motivated to recover because it was important to me that Justin knew who his father was. I wanted him to experience the joy of being in the clubhouse and sitting down for lunch with all the guys.

My rehab and recovery, which took two and a half years, were uneven and incredibly painful. But I never let anybody else tell me I couldn't continue to pitch. When my body let me know that I just couldn't do it, *then* I retired. On the day that I knew I'd play my final game, I had told Justin about it in advance. [Note: Kerry Wood walked off the mound to a standing ovation and was united with his then six-year-old son at the top of the dugout.] After the game, we spent most of that day together at Wrigley.

Sarah and I choose to remain in Chicago, in large part because the people of this city supported me through all my ups and downs. I believe the fans stood behind me because I never made excuses. We're happy to call Chicago home. I was always a Cub, I've always been a Cub, and I will continue to be a Cub.

*Kerry Wood was interviewed at the Wit Hotel in Chicago on January 10, 2013. His birthday is June 16, 1977.*

## Favorites

**BOOK**
*Lone Survivor: The Eyewitness Account of Operation Redwing and The Lost Heroes of SEAL Team 10* by Marcus Luttrell.

**MOVIE ABOUT BASEBALL**
*Bull Durham* (1988), directed by Ron Shelton. It's the comedic story of a minor league baseball team in Durham, North Carolina.

**PERFORMER**
Eddie Vedder of Pearl Jam.

**SONG**
"Harvest Moon" by Neil Young.

**QUOTATION**
"Adversity doesn't build character; it reveals it."
– AUTHOR UNKNOWN, BUT THE ADAGE WAS A FAVORITE OF PITCHING COACH OSCAR ACOSTA

"Adversity doesn't build character; it reveals it."